Christian Leadership

Principles & Practice

Roger Smalling

faithbook

CHRISTIAN LEADERSHIP
Principles & Practice

ISBN-13: 978-0-9864127-4-5

Published by faithbook
20-22 Wenlock Rd, London N1 7GU, United Kingdom

faithbook is a London-based publishing house
committed to designing beautiful brands that glorify God,
and producing thought-provoking publications to help reach those who are lost.
Our mission is to equip, connect, and empower God's people to serve their clients
and represent Christ with integrity and excellence in the marketplace.

www.faithbook.ltd

Through Holymedia, our creative growth agency,
we aim to create mass communication dedicated to God.

www.holymedia.io

Contents

Preface

Most books on Christian leadership leave me frustrated. They seem compendiums of eloquent exhortations on character and commitment, often with a detailed exposition of 1 Timothy 3. After perusing such books, I think, -Great material. But exactly what do I do?

Others seem Christianized management techniques, straight out of corporate America; wise sounding concepts but lacking soul, weak parodies of worldly administration.

Hopefully, I have avoided both extremes. A person who holds a high view of integrity and honor will have little need for exhaustive character studies. Without integrity, all the management techniques of Wall Street will not help them in ministry.

This is why I take my time in the first four chapters to nail down what a Christian philosophy of leadership is and is not. Hopefully, a deep sense of integrity and honor will be born in the reader.

These principles were born out of pain...the sorrow of seeing good people wounded by abusive leadership...the erosion of character of those in authority who refused to stand accountable for their actions...the anguish of watching leader colleagues end in humiliation.

Among many stresses of Christian ministry, the worst is laboring under incompetent leadership. Conversely, the greatest blessing a fledgling Christian worker can have is to serve under a godly mentor. Few have that privilege.

I wrote this book in the hopes that someday, because a future leader read this book, someone will say to him, 'it was a privilege to know you.'

About the author

D r. Roger Smalling has been in the ministry since 1964, when he went as a missionary to Europe with an independent mission. His leadership experience includes Field Leader for France, then later in South America as Team and Field Leader for Ecuador, as well as Assistant Regional Director for Latin America with that mission.

Later, while serving with the Presbyterian Church in America in Ecuador, he was instrumental in creating a successful leadership training system for the national Presbytery. This book was born out of that system.

Dr. Smalling served with *Ministries In Action* for twelve years as director of their Hispanic branch, under the title, "Visión R.E.A.L", an acrostic in Spanish for "Reformation In Latin America." This involved establishing and supervising leadership-training centers throughout Latin America. He currently cooperates with *Miami International Seminary* as a lecturer throughout Latin America.

Roger is married to Dianne, his wife of over 40 years. Together, they have authored ten books, available at:

www.smallings.com

PART ONE: Principles

Chapter 1

Christian Leadership Is Simple

This does not mean easy. We may follow all the right principles and things still not work out. Stressful situations develop. It can be hard work.

By 'simple' I mean the essential *principles* are easy to understand. They are also simple to apply if we have the moral courage to do so.

Christian leadership is not a mysterious domain for a chosen few with a special gift of wisdom. Even though you have no calling to a biblical office, the principles are available to all. This gives influence in the area of your gifts, with or without titles.

To those God has chosen for leadership, Paul says:

All Scripture is God-breathed and is useful for teaching, rebuking, correcting and training in righteousness, (17) so that the man of God may be thoroughly equipped for every good work. 2Timothy 3:16-17

THE POINT: Everything you need for effective Christian leader is in the Bible. Note Paul says, *thoroughly equipped.* You may not know *where* in the Bible to find a principle or recognize one when you see it. But it is *there.* That is why this course can be helpful.

Management paradigms in the business world change constantly. Christian organizations often publish or recommend books based on these paradigms. Why? Christians often fail to perceive the *biblical* paradigm.

To the degree you set up your organization or program to look like the corporate business world, is the degree to which you will find yourself resorting to the world's management principles. You will be unable to avoid them.

Books abound which are a hybrid of Christian principles and worldly management formulas. One reads these with a feeling of discomfort because the writers give the impression they are trying to mix oil and water.

Most of these are written by former businessmen who struggled to be Christian in the business world and managed it with some degree of success.

Then they get appointed to an office in the church and try to apply business principles under the assumption that what is good for business must be good for the church, while ignoring the inherent differences in philosophy and purpose between the two domains. [1]

The biblical philosophy of Christian leadership in ministry

The Bible teaches ONE philosophy of Christian leadership. Christ himself summarized and modeled it in Matthew 20. Principles of service and suffering form the basis of the leader's relationship to his subordinates while showing respect toward his ministerial colleagues as equals.

Christian leadership philosophy in the modern world is profoundly affected by current hierarchical management paradigms. Some Christian leadership books are merely warmed-over American business culture expressed in religious language. Christians successful in business leadership sometimes imagine they can incorporate their 'success' into the church and make God's Kingdom efficient...as though efficiency were the highest value in the Kingdom of God. [2]

Such approaches may indeed augment the efficiency of the church, but at the price of the same abuses in the business world. With their hierarchical mindset, they fail to see the forest for the trees.

Businessmen have often said, "If I ran my business like you run your church, I would be broke within a year." To this we may reply, "If I ran my church the way you run your business, I would end up with about as many sanctified people as you have in your business."

For this reason, we devote the first part of this section to differences between worldly and Christian philosophies of leadership. We illustrate how Christians sometimes incorporate the world's view of leadership, to their detriment.

Curiously, sectors of corporate business America have evolved unwittingly to a more Christian philosophy in their treatment of people. This has come about through decades of trial and error in managing people to keep them happy and productive in the workplace.

This has resulted in good literature on leadership and management techniques written by non-Christian businessmen. It is amusing to notice they consider their ideas original.

I have attempted to build a course that incorporates both theory and practice in an equal balance.

At the risk of appearing self-contradictory, some managerial techniques are in the latter portion of the course. These were chosen when helpful for applying a Christian principle and building relationships without being manipulative. They are not intended to endorse hierarchical authoritarianism in Christian organizations. People, not products, are the focus of God's Kingdom.

From this chapter we learn

- Christian leadership is fundamentally simple.

- The Bible recognizes **one** philosophy of Christian leadership, taught and modeled by Christ Himself.

-

God's word is sufficient for training in effective Christian leadership.

- Modern managerial techniques may be helpful if usable within a Christian view of leadership.

---

1. Ted Engstrom is the epitome of these. I do not recommend his books. 2. The glory of God is the highest value. Pleasing and honoring Him always takes precedence, even over apparent practicalities. Christ hinted at this in Mt 26:8-13, when a lady anointed Him with very expense perfume. A disciple complained it was a waste because it could have been sold and given to the poor. Jesus rejected this comment because He put the value of lady's motives, as well as His own honor, above the price of the perfume.

Chapter 2

The Foundation Virtue

West Point, the U.S. Army officer training college, is known for its strict code of honor. In response to any question, cadets may give only four answers: "Yes sir, No sir, I don't know sir, or No excuse sir." Making excuses is a crime. If a person under a cadet's responsibility makes a mistake, the cadet takes the blame. This is to teach them responsibility and honor and most of all, integrity.

One of these cadets graduated and was sent to Vietnam as a Lieutenant. His first assignment was to supervise the construction of a runway in the jungle that was already underway. A sergeant was in charge. Unfortunately, he knew nothing about runways. He asked the sergeant, "Are you sure the direction of this runway is correct?" The sergeant assured him it was. So the Lieutenant said, "Well, continue on therefore and I'll trust your judgment."

An hour and a half later, a Colonel came by who was an expert in runways and blared, "Who is the *idiot* who ordered this runway to be built in this direction?" The Lieutenant almost said, "This sergeant here, he said he knew...etc." But his actual words were, "I did, sir."

The Colonel got into the Lieutenant's face and asked, "Why did you order that?" The Lieutenant replied, "No excuse, sir."

At this moment the sergeant approached, with his hand upraised as thought to speak. The Colonel apparently deduced what had happened and asked the Lieutenant, "You just came out of West Point, didn't you?" The Lieutenant said, "Yes sir." The Colonel looked at the sergeant, then at the Lieutenant and said, "Well in that case, it was an honest mistake."

Later on the Colonel invited that Lieutenant to join his staff. This represented a substantial promotion. [1]

This true story illustrates the central virtue in leadership: *Integrity*. In the audio presentation on West Point leadership training from which this true story was taken, the lecturer said if they can teach a cadet to be a man of complete integrity, they can make him into a leader regardless of temperament or natural qualifications. They are prepared to fail men with natural leadership ability if they cannot infuse absolute integrity into his character.

The central virtue in leadership is integrity.

This concept is so associated with West Point that when the Colonel encountered an officer with absolute integrity, he assumed *West Point*.

Is this the kind of integrity we find in the leadership of our churches? If people meet a man of integrity today do they automatically assume he is evangelical?

God wants leaders to be men of integrity

Now this is our boast: Our conscience testifies that we have conducted ourselves in the world, and especially in our relations with you, in the holiness and sincerity that are from God. We have done so not according to worldly wisdom but according to God's grace. 13 For we do not write you anything you cannot read or understand. 2Corinthians 1:12,13

In this text, Paul declares he has no hidden agendas. He will not indulge in politicking nor does he plan to manipulate anyone. What you see is what you get. He means exactly what he says, nothing more. No need to examine the numerical value of the Greek letters to arrive at a hidden meaning.

The words used to translate *holiness and sincerity* in the above verse shows Paul means purity of motives and single-mindedness of purpose. [2] Transparency of this sort is simply a question of integrity and takes time to develop.

Integrity is so closely related to humility, we might argue they are synonyms. It would take a better philosopher than I to make such distinctions. Let us agree they are indispensably linked.

Integrity is central to all leadership, religious or secular. Business analysts, such as Stephen Covey in his book, *Seven Habits of Effective People*, have recently 'discovered' the importance of character in business. This book has become a best seller. [3]

Covey notes, however, a disturbing shift in attitudes toward character in leadership in western culture over the last 200 years. He classifies this shift as Character Ethic versus Personality Ethic.

In the first 150 years of the history of the United States, philosophy of leadership emphasized the importance of traits like integrity, humility, fidelity, etc. Since World War Two, the emphasis has been on personality traits as the key to success rather than ethics, per se. He notes:

> Success became more a function of personality, of public image, of attitudes and behaviors, skills and techniques... Other parts of the personality approach were clearly manipulative, even deceptive, encouraging people to use techniques to get other people to like them... [4]

Christians need to be aware of cultural shifts like this and carefully distinguish them from the traits Jesus calls for in those He chooses for leadership.

In his book *Good to Great*, researcher Jim Collins presents his analysis of companies that grew from good to great and stayed there. He found a quality in common among the leaders of these companies that had nothing to do with temperament:

> We were surprised, shocked really, to discover the type of leadership required for turning a good company into a great one.... Self-effacing, quiet, reserved, even shy- these leaders

are a paradoxical blend of personal humility and professional will. [5]

Note the point: The key quality in common among leaders of companies who had moved from good to great was *humility*. He adds,

> [These] leaders channel their ego needs away from themselves and into the larger goal of building a great company. It's not that [these] leaders have no ego or self-interest. Indeed, they are incredibly ambitious- but their ambition is first and foremost for the institution, not themselves. [6]

Leadership of lasting value cannot exist without this virtue. Management, yes. Manipulation and control yes...but not a true leadership that earns the loyalty of others at the cost of pain to oneself. It is the integrity of Jesus.

This is the Christian philosophy of leadership. There is none other.

The Caiaphas principle

Caiaphas was a man who sold his integrity for the price of peace. He was the high priest who presided over the trial of Jesus. In John 11:49,50 we read:

You know nothing at all! You do not realize that it is better for you that one man die for the people than that the whole nation perish.

In Caiaphas' perspective, it was better to abandon his integrity by condemning an innocent man than risk widespread destruction by attracting the attention of their Roman overlords. Was he right?

Yes, in the short run. He successfully averted Roman intervention and national disaster. He must have considered himself profoundly wise.

The long run, however, was different. Eventually the Romans came and destroyed the nation anyway. He won in the short run but lost everything in the end, including his own honor.

Jesus, on the other hand, seemed to lose in the short run. He was humiliated, crucified and seemed to disappear. Who is King of Kings today and where is Caiaphas?

Suppose you have a man in church caught in deep sin. You know you must discipline him. He is a very popular person, however, with wealth and influence. If you discipline him, it may divide the church. You might lose your job as pastor. What do you do?

This is a classic test of integrity. If you stand your ground, you may lose in the short run. The church might indeed be divided. You could lose your job. But God will give you far more than you ever lost, and you will have no regrets.

A final example

At a meeting of my Presbytery, the moderator asked for a report from the Missions Committee. The secretary of the committee rose and explained he did not have the report because he was unaware it would be required at the meeting.

Immediately the moderator began to reproach the secretary for his negligence. Toward the back of the assembly, one of the pastors, stood and said, "Sir, I am the chairman of the Missions Committee.

If there is any mistake, I am the one to blame and you may address any reproaches to me."

The moderator asked him if he knew about the error. He replied, "No sir, but that is beside the point. I am the person in charge, and if there is any reproach to be made, you may address it to me." The moderator dropped the point and continued with other business.

I thought, "It is no wonder this pastor has a thousand people in his church." Like the proverbial lamp on a hill, such integrity cannot be hidden.

Integrity, which includes humility, is the foundation virtue of leadership. Without it, a 'leader' is no more than a manager at best and a manipulator and controller at worst. Even the worldly notice this.

From this chapter we learn

- Integrity, sometimes called humility, is essential to Christian leadership.

- This virtue includes:

  ◦ Taking responsibility for the actions of one's subordinates.

  ◦ Standing for right even when it is costly, knowing God will reward in the long run.

Study Questions for Chapter TWO

1. Do you agree that integrity is the foundation virtue of Christian leadership? Justify your answer.

2. Explain the dilemma of the "Caiaphas Principle". Give an example from your own experience.

3. How could the example of the West Point Lieutenant be applied in a Christian context?

SUGGESTED STUDY: Read the first three chapters of Oswald Sanders' book and answer the questions connected with the first study. This book is an
excellent supplement that deals in depth with the character aspects of Christian leadership.

1. This anecdote is taken from a cassette tape series on West Point Leadership, which may be found in your local library. West Point Leadership: Making Leaders. West Point Lectures: West Point, VA, 1989.
2. The Greek words are haploteti and eilikrineia. The first refers to singleness of purpose. The second, to sincerity of motive. Together these show Paul's "no hidden agendas" conduct toward others.
Thayer's Lexicon, New Testament Greek-English Lexicon. ARCHA Publishers: Lafayette, IN 1979 pp. 55 and 175
3. Covey, Stephen. Seven Habits of Effective People. Simon and Schuster: New York, 1990. p. 14
4. Ibid. p.15
5. Collins, Jim. Good To Great. Harper: New York, 2001 pp. 22
6. Ibid pp. 21

Chapter 3

The Philosophy of Christian Leadership

Matthew 20:20-28

In the scenario described in Matthew Chapter 20, the mother of James and John approached Jesus asking that her sons sit beside Jesus in His Kingdom. This episode provided the opportunity for Jesus to introduce three key attitudes in Christian leadership: Suffering, Parity and Service.

SUFFERING: The pressures of leadership are enormous. A leader must be prepared to suffer, often in secret, to fulfill his calling.

PARITY: Ministers are equal in authority in the body of Christ. They relate to one another like knights at a round table rather than ranks in an army. Biblical government is an association of ministers, working together in mutual respect as equals. Complex authoritarian hierarchies have no place in God's Kingdom, are worldly in their conception and lead to the very things for which Jesus rebuked these two disciples. (We'll see more about hierarchism in the next chapter.)

SERVICE: Leaders have a *servant* rather than a *ruler* attitude. People are the whole point of their work, not tools toward their own purposes.

What were James and John seeking and how did they go about it? They sought status and honor through manipulation. They assumed the Kingdom of God would be set up just like any other government, with Jesus as supreme ruler, followed by a series of ranks. Notice they mentioned nothing of actual *work* to accomplish, just ranks.

We can imagine them plotting, "You know, Jesus can be a little tough on us sometimes. He's really gentle with women, though. Let's see if we can get Mama to talk to Him and maybe work out a good deal for ourselves."

This is politicking and manipulation, standard procedure in the world's leadership paradigm. Notice Jesus does not rebuke them for ambition, because ambition is a good thing if it is for God's glory. He admonishes against seeking one's own honor.

Jesus also makes it clear He is not in charge of promotions in the personnel department. The Father is. (V.23) They were asking the wrong person.

From this, we see a hint of the first principle of Christian leadership in the New Testament: It is a gift from God.

Nevertheless, these sons of Zebedee had two good qualities, although seriously misdirected:

AMBITION: This is a good characteristic for a Christian if the ambition is directed toward the glory of God rather than our own sense of self-worth.

CONFIDENCE: Unfortunately, it was confidence in them selves rather than in God. *We are able.* They considered themselves eminently *able*. The garden of Gethsemane taught them otherwise. They abandoned Jesus and fled.

This brings up the first key attitude Jesus taught them.

First key attitude: Suffering

> *But Jesus answered and said, 'You do not know what you ask. Are you able to drink the cup that I am about to drink, and be baptized with the baptism that I am baptized with?' They said to Him, 'We are able.'* Matt. 20:22

The call to Christian leadership is a call to suffering. The 'suffering' involved, especially in the western world, usually takes the form of psychological pressures and stresses other believers neither bear nor understand.

Frequently people have high expectations of a leader. They may be looking to a pastor to meet their needs rather than to Christ. When the pastor fails to meet their personal expectations, they may consider him incompetent.

Some under his care may be intractable and will only submit when pressured into it. Sometimes the leader must hold the line on godly principles, risking the misunderstanding and criticism of others.

Occasionally church leaders must apply biblical discipline when it may be unpopular to do so. When dealing with a disciplinary case, the leaders often cannot reveal the problem to the congregation. Members with incomplete knowledge of the case may draw wrong conclusions about the leaders' decisions. They may imagine the leaders are too harsh or too lax in discipline. The leaders may find themselves suffering in silence. God has wisely arranged it so.

Titles and honors that accompany the office of leader are insufficient to compensate for the stress.

Those who highly value titles or honors more than the service entailed, soon find themselves disappointed and disillusioned.

Similarly, in his book, **BROTHERS, WE ARE NOT PROFESSIONALS**, John Piper attacks the attitude of *professionalism* in pastoral ministry which puts aside the embracing of suffering as requisite:

> We pastors are being killed by the professionalizing of the pastoral ministry. The mentality of the professional is not...the mentality of the slave of Christ. Professionalism has nothing to do with the essence and heart of the Christian ministry... For there is no professional childlikeness (Matthew 18:3); there is no professional tenderheartedness (Ephesians 4:32); there is no professional panting after God (Psalms 42:1). [1]

Second key attitude: Parity

Jesus called them together and said, 'You know that the rulers of the Gentiles lord it over them, and their high officials exercise authority over them. Not so with you. Instead, whoever wants to become great among you must be your servant,' Matt. 20:25

On a certain mission field, I worked with a newly ordained national who happened to be a medical doctor. He had some rough edges to his personality...a bit independent and opinionated. We became great friends and worked well together. Let's call him 'José'.

Eventually, José moved to another city to work with a team. A missionary on the team called me and asked, "Roger, I'm having trouble getting along with José. I noticed you get along with him and work productively together. Can you give me some clues as to how to handle him?"

This was my answer: "Brother, in the first place, quit trying to 'handle' him. Treat him as a colleague. Call him up once in a while and ask his advice. Ask him to help you. Think of him as your equal because after all, he has the same ordination as you.

The missionary paused for about twenty seconds on the phone, thinking seriously. Then replied, "I don't think I can do that."

To this I answered, "Then I cannot help you."

This missionary could not consider any national, even a medical doctor, his equal. He saw himself on the rung of a hierarchy with all nationals on a lower rank.

Treating José, as an equal would have contradicted his entire leadership mind set, inherited from his North American corporate business culture.

Ironically, I had used the term *equal* to avoid saying I thought José was the better man! (It never occurred to me to think of a medical doctor of any nationality as inferior.) The relationship between the two lasted less than a year before José went elsewhere.

Tip: If you treat a man as an equal, assuming he is wise, he will defer to you in areas he knows you are knowledgeable.

Authoritarianism and hierarchism support each other, and it is hard to tell which is the driving force. Do authoritarian people create hierarchies? Dictatorial attitudes produce authoritarianism?

Regardless, authoritarianism is a byproduct of arrogance. Authoritarian people often suppose their superior office proves they are inherently superior individuals. This is why they *lord it over* others. They assume they have a natural right to do so.

Complex hierarchies are inevitable in the world. Armies are hierarchies, with their generals at the top, followed by colonels, majors, captains, and sergeants, down to privates. Likewise, it is with corporations. The CEO is at the top, followed by vice presidents, department managers, all the way down to stock boys in the basement.

Hierarchies are necessary in such domains. Jesus is not teaching that authoritarian hierarchies are wrong. He is simply saying, *"Not so with you."*

The phrase, *"Not so with you"*, is literally in Greek, "It shall not be so among you." Jesus was speaking in Aramaic, a dialect of Hebrew. In that language, future tenses are used as imperatives. Jesus was probably saying, "I forbid you to put into office people with authoritarian attitudes and temperaments."

This excludes some "natural" leaders from Christian offices. Christian organizations often ignore this principle. Along comes a person with natural leadership traits. Sure, he is a bit arrogant. He likes to control. Maybe he's a bit overbearing at times, but so what? He has *"leadership"*. So he gets authority in the organization. Result: Wounded people. Good people are lost who refuse to be the brunt of his arrogance.

Just because a man has natural leadership ability does not mean he should be a leader in a Christian organization.

If he tends toward authoritarian and controlling attitudes, he is the *last* person to be qualified. In their ranks, he must never be allowed to rise above the last one. Controllers must be controlled.

This may be what Jesus meant when he said, *"whoever wants to become great among you must be your servant."* Some scholars have interpreted this phrase to mean, "Servant leadership is the way to get promoted in the Kingdom of God." This interpretation may be valid. Considering the context, however, it seems more likely a prohibition against appointing people with authoritarian attitudes.

The point: Neither natural leadership ability nor experience in business or the military, nor profiles on a psychological test, are final indications a man should be a candidate for Christian leadership. If he holds autocratic attitudes, thinks hierarchically or tends to use or abuse people, he is disqualified as a candidate, regardless of other considerations.

Third key attitude: Service

...just as the Son of Man did not come to be served, but to serve and to give his life a ransom for many. Matthew 20:28

Christian leadership focuses more on helping others than commanding them. It is a life given over to service.

Many are attracted to Christian offices for the honors but wind up as negligent leaders, more concerned for their status than the welfare of the people. These do harm to themselves as well. (Ecclesiastes 8:9) *There is a time in which one man rules over another to his own hurt.*

The goal of a Christian leader is to make his followers the best they can be. In fact, if he can train someone to replace him, this is the best leadership of all.

Servant leadership is essential in the Kingdom of God because of the end product. In the business world, people are a resource to produce material goods. People give time and energy to produce something for public consumption, such as automobiles, pencils or whatever.

God's Kingdom uses material resources to produce sanctified people. The world considers this a non-issue. After all, sanctification is difficult to define, something only God can measure. Sanctified people are what the ministry is all about.

Notice the title of this chapter is, "**The** Christian Philosophy of Leadership", not "**A** Christian philosophy..." This is deliberate. Christ taught **one** philosophy of leadership. He did not say, "Try my suggestions and if you don't like them, invent your own paradigm."

Christian leadership involves a set of attitudes different from worldly systems. Embracing the inevitable suffering, whether psychological or physical, helps a leader put his own motives into perspective. Serving others to help them reach their full potential and treating fellow ministers as equals is more than the mere duties of an office. It is a way of life.

From this chapter we learn

- There exists only one philosophy of leadership in the Bible, the one taught by Christ.

- Embracing suffering and service, along with an attitude of parity toward your fellow ministers are essential attitudes forming Christ's philosophy of leadership.

- Ambition is good, as long as the ambition is to see God glorified.

- Confidence is good as long as it is based on confidence in God.

- God the Father alone is in charge of promotions in His Kingdom. Neither politicking nor "influence" are means for obtaining them.

- Jesus forbids his disciples to appoint to offices people with authoritarian attitudes.

- Neither leadership temperaments, psychological profiles nor experience in worldly hierarchies qualify a person for leadership in God's Kingdom.

Study Questions for Chapter Three

1. What are the three fundamental attitudes Christ requires of those who wish to lead in God's Kingdom?

2. In your own experience, what are some of the sufferings that come upon those in Christian leadership?

3. Describe what is meant by *parity* in a Christian context.

4. Describe some of the differences in goals between the world's leadership philosophy and that of the Kingdom of God.

5. Which part of this chapter was new to you? Or which was most interesting to you and why?

SUGGESTED STUDY: Read chapters 4-7 of Sanders' book and answer the questions connected with the second study.

---

1. Piper, John. Brothers, We Are Not Professionals. p.1,2

Chapter 4

The Dangers of Hierarchism

Hierarchism is an organizational structure based on ascending ranks, like a ladder. The military is a hierarchical structure with generals, colonels, and sergeants, down to privates. Authority is entirely vertical with no accountability at the top. No number of privates could ever hold a general accountable for his actions. Blame is usually passed downward.

Large corporations are also structured hierarchies, with CEO's, vice presidents, department managers, and on down. Again, authority is always from the top down with no accountability at the top. Lower ranks usually take the blame for the errors of the management. Officers of hierarchies do not represent the will of their subordinates.

Biblical government is the opposite and fundamentally simple. Officers serve the people in a representative system. [1] When it comes to the relationship of "officers" to one another, such as in a Presbytery, [2] every member has equal voice and vote. There are no ranks, just differences in functions. If there is blame, it accrues to the group as a whole.

The difference between the two is comparable to a ladder versus a round table. The entire structure is different because the goals and purposes are dissimilar.

When Christian organizations attempt to mimic the world's structures, the central principles Christ taught tend to be strangled. People become lost in a maze of bureaucracy as a monolithic organizational machine feeds itself rather than the people, focusing on its own existence as though it had intrinsic value.

During 35 years of ministry, principally in missions, I have observed many Christian organizations. Comparing these observations with other experienced ministers confirms the effects of hierarchism in a Christian context.

A missionary from another denomination came to me in a state of emotional distress. A few of the national pastors had told him in private they were considering withdrawing their churches from the denomination because of the incompetence of the mission field leader. He explained if he reported this to the field leader, it was likely the leader would accuse him of slander and being the cause of the problem. This leader was a close friend with the higher mission officials. I gave the missionary a suggestion as to how to deal with it and the matter was eventually resolved. [3]

By modeling the world's structures, Christians may forget to consider a central aspect of biblical theology...the corrupt nature of man. In structuring a Christian organization the principle issue is not efficiency but sanctification.

Dictatorship is the most efficient form of government known to man. That is why dictators are hard to defeat. Dictators dehumanize people, depriving them of the free expression necessary to reflect God's image. It is the straight line between two points but casualties are strewn along its wake. Hitler's Germany is a glaring example in the political realm.

In the religious domain, we saw a reformation in Europe fought over the dictatorial authority of Catholicism. Church government, besides the doctrine of salvation, was a big issue.

To discern the morality of a leadership structure, one should ask what it stimulates...the Agamic nature or the new nature in Christ.

The Peter Principle: Mediocrity and incompetence

In his classic book, **THE PETER PRINCIPLE** [4], sociologist John Peters describes how each member of a hierarchy tends to rise to his level of incompetence. As a person performs well at one level, he may be promoted to the next, until he attains a position beyond his abilities. He will remain at this position generating problems for him and others. Meanwhile, many gifted people abandon ship. With time, incompetence of this sort multiplies until the organization as a whole becomes mediocre.

Good Christian leaders, functioning within a hierarchical system, try to mitigate these negative effects. These efforts are laudable, though often futile. Human nature, including among Christians, is susceptible to the temptations generated by hierarchical systems.

HIERARCHIES TEND TO STIMULATE THE WORST IN FALLEN HUMAN NATURE

This includes Christian hierarchies. Some of these aspects are:

ARROGANCE

People tend to want to feel superior to others. Hierarchies provide for this by giving ranks, one superior to the other. The assumption is, "I have a superior rank because I am a superior person."

UNHOLY AMBITION AND JEALOUSY

A person sees another in a rank above his and says to himself, "he is no better than I. In fact, I can do his job better. So why shouldn't I have that rank?"

DIRTY POLITICKING

If a person wants a superior rank, he may be tempted to try to pull strings and make deals to get it. This is morally questionable and wasteful of effort that could be spent in productive work.

The Apostle James notes in James 3:16:

For where you have envy and selfish ambition, there you find disorder and every evil practice.

The term *evil practice* translates *phaeton pram*, literally "foul business." [5] The modern phrase, "dirty politicking" expresses it well.

BLAME SHIFTING

This is a form of moral cowardice. Human nature has a tendency to blame a subordinate when something goes wrong. Blame shifting was Adam's first reaction after the fall. (Genesis Chapter Three)

Imagine a man carrying a load up a ladder. If the man on the top drops his load, where does it go? On the man beneath, who dumps it on the man below him. The guy on the bottom gets the full load. In a hierarchy, the load is the *blame*.

MAN-PLEASING

Since a person's rank in the hierarchy depends on the good will of the rank above him, this tempts him to focus on pleasing the man above rather than pleasing God.

LOSS OF COMPETENT PERSONNEL

According to Dr. Peters in *The Peter Principle*, hierarchies tend to squeeze out those who question the way things are done, even if they are highly competent. [6]

A hierarchy, like any organism, becomes more focused on perpetuating its own existence than to what it was created to produce. People who rock the boat will be thrown out of that boat. It does not matter if they were among the few doing the rowing.

DISREGARD OF THE SPIRITUAL AUTHORITY OF ORDAINED OFFICES

I mention this one last for emphasis, not because it is least important. It is the most serious problem generated by authoritarian structures. In a Christian hierarchy, leaders sometimes act as though their man-made title or ranks negates the spiritual authority of biblical ones. The Word of God accords certain rights and privileges to all ordained officers in the body of Christ. Hierarchical structures overlook these. See Chapter Eight for more on this.

What if you are a leader in an authoritarian Christian hierarchy?

With a little imagination, you can implement administrative devices to minimize the damage; though doing so requires a rare moral courage. Why courage? These strategies require accountability to the people you lead. [7]

Examples:

PERIODIC EVALUATIONS OF YOUR LEADERSHIP

Have it in writing and anonymous by the people you lead. This gives subordinates the opportunity to say what they really think and do so safely. In this way, you will get the truth about your leadership style.

CREATE AN ANONYMITY COMMITTEE

This may consist of two or three people who can receive complaints about problems without revealing the sources. If there are enough complaints about a particular leader, this can be brought to the attention of upper-level management before the leader is able to do serious damage. The reason this requires moral courage is because the leader in question might be you.

MEMOS TO SUBORDINATES ABOUT PROPOSED POLICIES ASKING FOR THEIR FEEDBACK

This gives people the feeling of participation in the decision process.

Tip: Do NOT insult the intelligence of your subordinates by announcing an "open door policy" unless they can hold you accountable for what you say or do to them inside the door. [8]

Any device that allows you to be vulnerable to your subordinates and accountable for your actions will gain respect and credibility. Ironically, once you have respect and credibility, those devices will likely become unnecessary.

> ANY DEVICE THAT ALLOWS YOU TO BE ACCOUNTABLE FOR YOUR ACTIONS WILL GAIN RESPECT AND CREDIBILITY

Are you joining a Christian organization?

A good way to discern if the organization is authoritarian is to ask them, "In what way can you be made to stand accountable for the way you treat subordinates?" Or, "If an employee becomes the victim of an administrative abuse, what resources does he have for redress of grievances?" If you get no clear answer, look for another organization.

Summary

Authoritarian hierarchism is unbiblical for Christian organizations or churches. It stimulates latent tendencies in our fallen nature. Christian leaders need to be aware of these tendencies and do what they can to minimize them. This may require an uncommon moral courage and commitment to the fundamental principle of absolute integrity in making ourselves vulnerable and accountable to those we lead.

From this chapter we learn

- Authoritarian hierarchism is a worldly form of organizational structure, antithetical to the leadership principles Christ embodied.

- Authoritarian hierarchism stimulates the worst in human nature, leading to arrogance, selfish ambition, politicking, blame shifting and more.

- Christian leaders involved in such structures can mitigate the damage if they have the courage to do so, by instituting administrative devices to make themselves vulnerable and accountable to those they lead.

Study Questions for Chapter Four

1. Explain here whether you think it is possible for a Christian authoritarian hierarchy to avoid generating the problems described in this chapter.

2. Invent another administrative device, other than those mentioned in the chapter for mitigating the negative effects of hierarchism.

3. Explain the Peter Principle.

SUGGESTED STUDY: Read chapters 8-10 of Sanders' book and answer the questions connected with the third study.

1. Since I am Reformed, I consider Reformed, or Presbyterian government to be the only biblical form. This is what I mean when I use the term 'biblical government.'

2. A Presbytery is a council of ministers and elders representing associated churches in a region or large city. It meets to deal with matters in common. The term is derived from the Greek term PRESBITERION, used 1 Timothy 4:4.

3. The suggestion I gave was to have the nationals confront the field leader as per Mt 18:15-18 and then write a letter to the mission headquarters.

4. This entertaining little book is must read for anyone trying to understand how hierarchies can become so incompetent.

5. Accordance Bible Software. Oaktree Company: Temecula, CA, 1999

6. ibid, p.69

7. Usually organizations insist they are accountable. What they normally mean by this is that they are accountable to someone above them in rank, but not responsible to anyone below. This is not "accountability" in the sense we mean it here.

8. An "open door policy" means telling your subordinates they are welcome to come into your office and discuss any of their concerns. Most people will have sense enough to ignore leaders who say this.

Chapter 5

Functional Aspects of Leadership

The great myth of Christian leadership

When God wants a leader, He looks down over a group of brothers and chooses the one with a special gift of wisdom, along with a profound spirituality. This is why God chooses some and not others.

The above paragraph is a myth.

I have known leaders who actually believed the above. I have observed two points in common among them: First, all were under forty years old. Second, all of them made fools of themselves.

Perhaps the age of forty is a coincidence. Maybe not. I would never disqualify a man merely because he is under the age of forty. Possibly this number of years gives a man time to discover his own weaknesses, get a few lumps on his head and learn the humility which comes from a more accurate self-knowledge.

The term *elder* in Scripture derived its meaning from the maturity normally associated with years of experience. Regardless of a man's age, we expect him to possess the wisdom, maturity and humility of an *elder*.

The point: Promotion to leadership is a gift of God's grace. No one ever fully deserved it. The Apostle Paul said,

> *But by the grace of God I am what I am, and his grace to me was not without effect. No, I worked harder than all of them — yet not I, but the grace of God that was with me.* 1Corinthians 15:10

Did Paul, therefore, deserve to be an Apostle? No. It was the grace of God alone who called and qualified him. There is no function in the Kingdom of God we are big enough for without his grace. [1]

The gift of leadership

The Bible indicates Christian leadership is a gift of the Spirit.

> *We have different gifts, according to the grace given us... (8)...if it is leadership, let him govern diligently;...* Romans 12:6-8

Although the spiritual gift of leadership may accompany a natural gift, God is not dependent on natural human talents. He calls some to it despite reluctance on their part. Moses was an example of this. His first reaction was to make excuses for rejecting the call. (Ex.3:11,12)

The phenomenon of spiritual authority

Defining spiritual authority is like pinning down the meaning of *anointing*. We may not know what it is, but we sure know what it isn't!

Spiritual authority is the testimony of God about the authenticity of a leader, along with the conviction that one ought to esteem to his ministry.

This is what was taking place when the Father spoke to the disciples about Jesus,

This is my Son, whom I have chosen; listen to him. Luke 9:35 [2]

———— ◄◊► ————

SPIRITUAL AUTHORITY IS THE TESTIMONY OF GOD ABOUT THE AUTHENTICITY OF A LEADER

———— ◄◊► ————

H ave you ever had the experience of meeting a Christian leader, such as at a Bible study or church and suddenly you get the sense you should listen to that man as approved by God and do as he says? You may be unsure of why you feel that way, but you know it is God's confirmation.

THAT is spiritual authority. It is an anointing for leadership. It is neither the product of leadership techniques nor appointments to offices, nor a personality trait. It is the product of a divine anointing which transcends all these.

A PARADOX: Although spiritual authority is of grace, it is nevertheless costly to obtain. It takes service and suffering, along with personal discipline and a private devotional life only you and God know about.

Now, let's take a look at some of the functions of a Christian leader.

The leader's function

Keep watch over yourselves and all the flock of which the Holy Spirit has made you overseers. Be shepherds of the church of God, which he bought with his own blood. Acts 20:28

This verse is perhaps the richest description of the Christian leader's responsibility in the entire Bible. Note these particulars:

THE LEADER'S FIRST CONCERN MUST BE FOR HIS OWN SPIRITUAL WELFARE

This sounds surprising but it is true. *Keep watch over yourselves* means the leader is to attend to his own spiritual welfare first. He must carefully maintain a solid and consistent devotional life. A chief trap of Satan is to get us so busy we neglect prayer and fellowship with God through the Word. Many a leader has fallen because he has gotten so busy in the ministry, he has neglected his own soul and left himself an easy target for the enemy.

THE LEADER'S FIRST CONCERN MUST BE HIS OWN SPIRITUAL WELFARE

THE CALLING IS FROM GOD

Though we qualify to be ordained in Christian organizations, in the final analysis, it is the Spirit who makes us *overseers*.

The term, be shepherds in Acts 20:28 translates the Greek verb POIMAINO. This verb means, to lead, with the implication of providing for — "to guide and to help, to guide and take care of." It also means, to rule, with the implication of direct personal involvement. [3]

Notice the term definitely includes authority. A Christian leader is not there merely to make suggestions. He has authority from God to be directly involved in the personal lives of the sheep. He feeds the sheep by providing them the Word of God.

Bought with his own blood. Paul adds this to emphasize the supreme value and importance of spiritual leadership.

No occupation or function in the world could possibly be more important because nothing else could cost a higher price than the blood of Christ.

In short, the leader's function is to shepherd. People are more important than programs, plans or procedures. In our present technological society, we may easily lose sight of this central fact.

The leader's strategy

It was he who gave some to be apostles, some to be prophets, some to be evangelists, and some to be pastors and teachers, 12 to prepare God's people for works of service, so that the body of Christ may be built up. Eph.4:11,12

Training the church to do the work of the ministry is the leader's strategy.

Who does the work of the ministry according to the text above? God's people. The church members. Everyone in the church should have a job. The leader's role is to be a supervisor. That's what "bishop" means. He is "overseer" or "supervisor." (Gk. *Episcopes:* The prefix *Epi* means "upon" and *skopos* means "look." It refers to one who watches over the activities of another.)

Suppose you were looking for a construction crew to build your house. You go to a construction site where you have heard a crew is working. There, you notice a group of workers standing around in a circle, shovels in hand, with a supervisor in the middle. The supervisor is digging laboriously. All the workers are applauding and saying, "Go, boss! Keep up the good work. You're doing a fine job!"

What would you think of a crew like that? Would you want them to build your house?

TRAINING THE CHURCH TO DO THE WORK OF THE MINISTRY IS THE LEADER'S STRATEGY

U nfortunately, many churches function this way. The church sits and applauds while the pastor does all the preaching, teaching, visitation, counseling and correcting. They praise his efforts and it never occurs they should be doing any of those things.

No wonder pastors suffer such a high percentage of heart attacks.

A man once asked me what I thought was the ideal pastor. I answered, "The ideal pastor is one who could enter the church on a Sunday morning, sit in the back row the entire service and do absolutely nothing." The man looked at me puzzled until I explained how such an ideal pastor would have trained others in the church to do everything he can do. Someone would lead the service. Another would do the announcements. Another would preach, etc.

A classic trap for the fledgling leader is to focus on the weakest members rather than the strongest. After all, they seem the most needy. The discerning leader spends his time preparing the strong to help the weak. The big danger for the novice leader is assuming his job is to heal all the wounded, sooth all the hurt feelings, and support the weak. (This is like trying to feed all the poor, which Jesus said is impossible. It never ends.)

Such a trap duplicates a fundamental teaching error sometimes committed in the public schools, [4] lowering your standards to accommodate the weakest student. The result is poor education.

If a leader has the wisdom to invest in *potential* people, rather than *problem* people, he will discover he is training those who can minister to the problem people.

Years ago in Ecuador, I was doing a church plant in a suburb of Quito. Each church has its own personality, just like individuals do. This church had the personality of a lazy plow horse. If we stopped exhorting, it would just stop and go to sleep.

One Sunday, I was preaching a serious exhortatory sermon when I realized most of the congregation was looking out the side door. I stopped, leaned over to see what they were looking at, and noticed a cat playing with a ball.

I was shocked. They were more interested in a cat than in the warnings in God's word toward them. Then I noticed four members taking notes. For their sake, I finished the sermon.

At home that afternoon, I determined to prepare no more sermons for the congregation. All my sermons would be for those four people only. It turned out this was the wisest decision I could have made. One of those four was a young man who later started his own church with 150 members.

Prepare your messages for those who take you seriously. Prepare the strong to help with the weak.

The leader's principal product

*And the things you have heard me say in the presence of many
witnesses entrust to reliable men who will also be qualified to
teach others.* 2Timothy 2:2

The main thing a Christian leader should produce is other *leaders.* That is
how Paul's friend Timothy ended up in the ministry.

Some pastors seem reluctant to prepare other men in their congregation for
leadership. Having known many pastors, I suspect some fear others may
rise to take their place and they would be out of a job. Rather than take the
risk, they prefer the congregation as a whole remain mediocre.

THE MAIN PRODUCT OF CHRISTIAN LEADERSHIP IS OTHER LEADERS

E vangelist Leighton Ford noted how some strong leaders fail to
develop the leadership under them, with long-term disastrous results:

> Perhaps some of the first-generation leaders saw the
> second-generation leaders as unwelcome competitors and
> did not set out to develop them. An Indian proverb says,
> "Nothing grows under a Banyan tree." often the shadow of
> these strong leaders was so large that the little seedlings were
> not nurtured under them. [5]

Observation and experience shows God promotes to greater ministry leaders who prepare others to take their place.

Summary

The call to leadership comes from God by grace. No one ever deserves it. The leader is first committed to people rather than a program. His strategy is to prepare others to do the ministry including training others to lead.

From this chapter we learn

- God's choice of leaders is based on His grace, not on any special wisdom a candidate possesses.

- The leader's function is to shepherd the people of God.

- The leader's strategy is to train the people to do the work of the ministry.

- The leader's principal product is other leader.

Study Questions for Chapter Five

1. What is the great myth about Christian leadership and why is it a myth?

2. What is the leader's function and what does it entail?

3. What is the leader's strategy? How can you apply it?

4. What is the leader's primary product?

5. What is the common trap mentioned in this chapter? How can you avoid it?

SUGGESTED STUDY: Read chapters 11-14 of Sanders' book and answer the questions connected with the fourth study.

1. This is a quote from Dr. Paul Kooistra, at the time, director of Mission to the World during a mission conference in July 2002.

2. The command "listen to him" in Aramaic carries the meaning, 'obey what he says.'

3. The clause "be shepherds" translates the verb, poimaino. Louw and Nida comment:

poimai÷nw : a figurative extension of meaning of poimai÷nwa "to shepherd," 44.3) "to lead," with the implication of providing for — "to guide and to help, to guide and take care of." e˙k souv ga»r e˙xeleu/setai hJgou/menoß, o¢stiß poimaneiˆ˚ to\n lao/n mou to\n ∆Israh/l "from you will come a leader who will guide and help my people Israel." Mt 2:6.

37.57 poimai÷nw: to rule, with the implication of direct personal involvement — "to rule, to govern." poimaneiˆ˚ aujtou\ß e˙n rJa¿bdw^ sidhra◊^ "he will rule them with an iron rod" Rev 2:27.

4. I can say this from my experience as a former public school teacher.

5. Ford, Leighton. Transforming Leadership. p.24

Chapter 6

The essentials

From where does a vision come from? How do we implement it?

To answer these questions, we must take a look at three leadership styles often found in Christian circles: Pioneers, a Manager and Janitors. This list is not exhaustive. Others exist. Some individuals may be a mixture.

PIONEERS have a vision for something new. He is the trailblazer, taking the risks to go where nobody has gone before or do something in a new place. He has enthusiasm, drive and creativity. He is impervious to criticism and impatient with the petty people who play it safer.

Though pioneers are great for getting things going, they usually make poor administrators. This is because they have little patience for the minutia necessary in administration. They also tend to lose interest in projects once they are started, preferring to go on to something else.

MANAGERS follow in the footsteps of a pioneer, carrying forward the vision the pioneer has established. He puts order into the vision. Though he also owns the vision, he may be dissatisfied with the implementation. He sees more clearly the means to accomplish the goals.

JANITORS are conservative types who want to institutionalize the vision to maintain results are they are. In a church setting, these people tend to lack vision for anything new. We call them "Janitors" because their primary concern is to see everything is kept clean and safe. If the congregation is morally clean, with sound doctrine and committed to the status quo, they are content.

They spend time dealing with disciplinary cases, discontent people or people with deep problems. Leadership development is not their priority. They perceive themselves as spiritual leaders because they have success dealing with these types of problems. It is questionable if they may be called leaders at all.

They tend to resist new projects because they themselves have no compelling goals. Their focus is keeping everyone happy so that they stay in the church. If spiritual janitors are allowed primary leadership in the church, it is highly unlikely the church will grow numerically.

What is vision?

Vision is an attainable dream. It involves two aspects:

- A dream

- A workable plan

This means a goal of great value, difficult to attain, requiring long-term investment of time and personnel.

VISION IS AN ATTAINABLE DREAM

B oth must exist to qualify as *vision*. A plan without a dream lacks the momentum to attract the necessary leaders to make it work. A dream without a plan is merely visionary and never gets off the ground.

The Protestant Reformation was the result of the vision of several men like Luther, Calvin and Knox. It was a goal of immense value, costing many lives over three generations. The religious freedom and prosperity many countries enjoy today is the direct result of that vision.

In the political domain, the Latin American revolution under Simon Bolivar was the result of a vision. Bolivar dreamed of the liberation of an entire continent. It was costly and required a lifetime investment of resources. A continent was worth it.

A vision need not be as ambitious as the above examples. Every successful church or Christian organization was started by a person with the vision to see it happen.

A vision without a plan is merely visionary

Listening to a visionary may be entertaining but so are movies.

Eloquence does not equal vision, either. Certain articulate and intelligent people discourse eloquently about what needs to be done. They seem more adept at analyzing the deficiencies of others than creating workable plans. Though they appear knowledgeable and confident, one never quite grasps exactly what they are saying. It is like catching smoke. (Politicians are often like that.) These are visionaries at best and leaders, not at all...windbags to be ignored.

A dream and a plan is not quite enough

Some may have a dream and a plan and still not be leaders. A third element must enter in; the personal drive and commitment to implement it. Without this, all they will only be trying to persuade others to do the work.

A dream and a plan without "drive" is like a sports car with a driver who won't turn on the key.

Elements of a sensible vision

SIMPLICITY

You must be able to explain your vision in a few seconds. Otherwise, it is too complex. People need to understand it to support it. Your promotional literature should project the vision in the first line or two.

Slogans and acronyms help. If you can come up with a slogan this will help people grasp the idea. [1]

DIFFICULT BUT NOT IMPOSSIBLE

If it were easy, somebody would have already done it. If the goal is attainable and desirable, but has not been done, it is either because nobody believes it is possible or no one has the drive to attempt it.

Accomplishing a vision requires a person who can distinguish between *impossible* and *difficult*. The ability to take what others see as impossible and evolve a plan for doing it, distinguishes a Christian worker from a Christian leader.

THE ABILITY TO TAKE WHAT OTHERS SEE AS IMPOSSIBLE AND EVOLVE A PLAN FOR DOING IT, DISTINGUISHES A CHRISTIAN WORKER FROM A CHRISTIAN LEADER.

Characteristics of a godly vision

IT MUST ADVANCE THE KINGDOM OF GOD, NOT YOUR OWN SELF-ESTEEM

How does your vision advance the Kingdom of God and produce holy people? Remember, God's goal is to create a holy people for His Kingdom and glorify His name this way. Anything we do must fit into this goal or our idea did not come from God. Some have built their own empires as monuments to themselves in the name of God's Kingdom.

Others have a strong psychological need to affirm their own self-worth. Beware of motives.

IT MUST BE BASED ON A PERSONAL CALL FROM GOD

Just because it is a good idea does not necessarily mean it is God's call for us to accomplish it. David had a great idea for building a temple to honor God. Nathan the prophet informed him that God was pleased with the idea, but it was Solomon who was called do it.

Summary

Although the Bible teaches only one philosophy of Christian leadership, leadership styles may differ, depending on temperaments and circumstances. Some are pioneers, others managers or maintenance people. A leader is partly characterized by having the initial vision. A vision is an attainable and valuable dream that comes from God.

From this chapter we learn

- Some leaders are pioneers, others are managers and others maintenance people.

- A vision is an attainable dream of great lasting value, difficult to accomplish and requiring great expenditure in resources.

- A vision must be accompanied with a plan or it is simply visionary, leading nowhere.

- The vision must be simple enough for people to understand and get on board with it.

- The vision comes normally through a personal walk with God like any other calling.

- A genuine vision must advance God's Kingdom for His glory, not merely our own personal satisfaction.

Study Questions for Chapter Six

1. What are the three styles of leadership mentioned in this chapter? Which kind are you? Would you like to be different?

2. Define the term "vision".

3. What are the essential elements of a vision?

4. What would be a key characteristic of a visionary?

5. How does a believer receive from God a "vision" for his life and ministry?

SUGGESTED STUDY: Read chapters 15-18 of Sanders' book and answer the questions connected with the fifth study.

---

1. Hopefully, "Visión R.E.A.L" is an example of this. As any acronym, Reforma En America Latina sticks in the mind.

Chapter 7

Planning & Goal Setting

In this chapter, we will deal with planning on two levels...large and small. First, we will discuss the kind of plan you need for a large vision of the sort mentioned in Chapter Five. Then we will deal with simple yearly planning of a kind done in a local church setting.

Planning the vision

Suppose your vision is to establish the largest and most influential Christian school in the city. How would you go about creating a plan for it?

The success of your vision depends in large part on your ability to communicate it to potential participants and supporters. This in turn depends on your own ability to think through intermediate steps toward the goal and get a realistic grasp of the resources necessary.

It helps to write in a brief paragraph what is your vision. Make it simple. Afterwards, write out your intermediate goals and how you expect to attain them.

To convince mature Christians of the validity of your vision, your plan needs to incorporate certain ministerial elements, often found in missionary principles.

Elements of a good plan

You need to clarify in your plan:

How it will eventually be reproducible by the participants

This is a basic missionary principle. When the apostles established churches, they trained key men to do the same. An important question to ask is, "How much of what I am doing is reproducible by the people I am ministering to, using their own resources?"

How it will become self-sustaining

Part of the plan must be to make the ministry self-supporting. Otherwise, you will have created a system of dependency. This hinders Christian maturity. Make yourself dispensable.

If your vision requires your perpetual existence to make it work, then it is your own nest you are building, not God's Kingdom.

How you plan to obtain the necessary resources

Every successful Christian leader can tell how he started with next to nothing and how God supplied bit by bit. God will rarely put everything into our hands at once. God normally starts small. Look on each bit of resource as God's down payment on the vision.

What are your intermediate goals?

One of the most appealing devices for convincing people of the reality of your vision is intermediate goals. These are the stages you will pass through to accomplish your vision. Your first goal should be something obviously attainable, preferably something on which you have already made progress.

Example: What would be the effect on potential supports if you were able to say about your Christian School vision, "We have the property picked out and have made an initial down payment on it."

The psychological impact is staggering. It answers loud and clear the first question in their minds, "Is this guy serious?" It shows practical movement and initiative.

Tip: Put it all on paper

This helps clarify your own thinking as well as help measure progress. You can make the statement periodically, "We will know we are reaching our goal when..." Participants in the vision will see better where they fit. Also, as a Christian leader of integrity, you have nothing to hide.

Planning within the local church setting

In the local church, the leaders need to establish vision and goals. A church without a vision statement and clear goals will likely go nowhere. Annual planning is a must for a church.

Example: Suppose young families are moving into your community. Your goal is to reach for Christ five of these new families during the next year. You and your church board have embraced this challenge and announced this goal to the congregation. What now?

REVIEW THE GOAL

Ask your subordinates for their creative input. This helps them own the goal. Set fixed dates to review your "goal progress". If you have a goal for this year, for example, then set dates every two months to review results. This helps keep everyone on track.

BE PREPARED FOR OPPOSITION

There will always be dissenters, no matter what you do. Example: Your goal is win five young couples to the Lord. Then one Sunday someone approaches you in the church and says, "A group of us would like to start a ministry to the elderly in the nursing home." How should you respond?

You might say, "That's a laudable goal, but how does it fit in with our vision this year of incorporating five young couples into the church? Show me how your idea fits in with the vision of the church and we can approve it. Otherwise, no." Doing this helps your members stay focused on the task without getting sidetracked.

Problems inevitably spring up in the church that tend to absorb your time. Watch out for this.

Example: At the invasion of D-Day during World War II, everything that could go wrong, did. There were far more casualties than anticipated. But the generals gave the order to keep advancing. The allies won, despite errors and casualties.

A sample plan

Let's use a realistic example of a goal and plan:

DEFINE YOUR OBJECTIVES

The *objective* is the primary means to implement the vision.

In this illustration, the church leadership has decided to establish a school for about 300 students within 10 years. The school will be entirely self-supporting, requiring no resources from the church.

ESTABLISH INTERMEDIATE GOALS

An intermediate goal means the smaller steps necessary to arrive at the final objective. Some sample intermediate steps may be:

- Start with a day care center the first year to acquaint people in the neighborhood with the church. Start kindergarten using Sunday school rooms in the church building. Add one grade each successive year until the objective is reached.

- Recruit two teachers during the first year to be able to add a new grade the next year.

- Designate ten percent of the offerings to the school project to provide funds for next year and for a building fund.

LIST RESOURCES AVAILABLE

A gratifying part of implementing a God-ordained vision is watching how He provides. People often discover they have more resources available than they thought.

The church has two qualified grade school teachers available. The assistant pastor is a former school administrator and can function as chief administrator of the project in its beginning stages. Sunday school rooms can be used as classrooms for the first three years. Eight families in the church have preschoolers and have expressed interest in putting their kids into the project. The church has $10,000 aside for initial expenses.

The church owns enough property to expand with new buildings.

<hr />

A GRATIFYING PART OF IMPLEMENTING A GOD-ORDAINED VISION IS WATCHING HOW HE PROVIDES

<hr />

LIST RESOURCES LACKING

For completion of final objective, twenty qualified staff is needed. This will include teachers for all grade levels, a secretary, registrar and two administrators.

Financial needs: The project will need about $250,000 for new buildings and $50,000 for equipment within the next five years, to be able to accommodate grades five through eight.

REPRODUCTION

In the fifth year, we will begin to train interested teachers in school administration. This will free up the current administrators for starting a new school on the other side of town.

Summary

A good plan solidifies the vision. A brief outline of the plan lends credibility and comprehension to it. Intermediate goals make the long-term vision seem more attainable. A good plan includes ways to acquire the necessary resources.

In any plan, whether a larger vision or yearly planning in a church, there will always be dissenters and distracting problems. A good leader stays on track and does not allow these things to deviate him.

From this chapter we learn

- It is very helpful to put your vision in writing. A brief paragraph explaining the vision helps people grasp the central idea quickly.

- A good plan incorporates intermediate goals. This is how you measure progress. This includes plans for obtaining the necessary resources.

- Review progress with your subordinates regularly to keep on track.

- Do not allow problems or dissenters to deviate you from the goal.

Study Questions for Chapter Seven

1. Describe some elements of a good plan.

2. What are the benefits in writing out your vision and plans?

3. What is an intermediate goal? Give an example.

SUGGESTED STUDY: Read chapters 19-22 of Sanders' book and answer the questions connected with the sixth study

Chapter 8

Creative Thinking

A t a mission conference, the Sunday school teachers wanted all of the children to understand what a missionary does.

A couple of the teachers, however, objected. They felt the five and six year olds were too young to grasp the concept of missions.

The teachers conferred over the problem. One teacher had a shower curtain with a map of the world printed on it. During the conference, they took the shower curtain to the classes along with cans of shaving cream. They put some shaving cream on the part of the map representing the USA, along with a few other countries that send out missionaries.

The teachers said the cream represented the message about Jesus. They explained to the kids that those were the countries where the Gospel is preached. Then they asked the kids why there was no shaving cream on other countries. They explained something about the people in certain countries and that they did not have the Gospel. So somebody must take the Gospel to them. How?

They had the kids take off their shoes, step into the piles of cream, pick up some on their feet and walk it over to the countries in which there was none.

Toward the end of the conference, the pastor asked the five year olds, what is a missionary? The kids responded, "A missionary takes the message of Jesus to places where people don't have it."

Those teachers solved a problem some originally assumed impossible. They did it with creative thinking.

One of the key characteristics distinguishing genuine leaders from mere managers is creative thinking. It explains why some leaders seem content to maintain the status quo.

——◆O◆——

A KEY CHARACTERISTIC OF A LEADER IS CREATIVE THINKING

——◆O◆——

What is creative thinking?

We can define creative thinking as the ability to invent original ideas for accomplishing goals.

The source of creative thinking is our imagination. This is a faculty of mind given by God, which He expects us to use. Guidance from God often comes through the application of our own mental faculties.

Why are we not better at creative thinking?

LAZINESS

Thinking is hard work. Creative thinking is hardest of all. Just ask a novelist. Most will tell you they only write three or four hours a day because it is too exhausting. [1]

WRONG THEOLOGY ABOUT GUIDANCE

Christians sometimes have wrong concepts about the mind. They wait for God to give divine revelation, while God waits for them to use the faculties He gave them. Result: Nobody is moving and nothing gets accomplished.

REPRESSION OF CREATIVE FACULTIES

A high school teacher put a small dot on the blackboard. Then he asked the class what it was. The students all agreed that is was nothing but a dot of chalk on the blackboard. The teacher replied, "I did the same exercise yesterday with a group of children. One thought it was an insect egg or perhaps a bird's eye. Another thought it was the head of a bald man seen from an airplane."

Why the difference? In the years between kindergarten and high school students were discarding their imagination. Why? Because they were learning to be "specific" about things, learning the "right answers" and learning what is "realistic." [2]

Absorbing facts is not the same as exercising the mind. In some countries, the education system is based on rote memorization. Students write down verbatim what the teacher says, then copy it neatly into a notebook at home. This is supposed to be education. It is not education. It is brainwashing.

FEAR OF FAILURE OR RIDICULE

Nobody wants to make a fool of himself. The temptation toward this becomes stronger as we advance in leadership. We think, "If this idea fails, we'll look like fools and people will lose confidence in us."

NEGATIVE THINKING

What is the difference between a leader who gets things done and those who only manage the work of others? The former ignores the reasons why it can't be done and does it anyway.

Great entrepreneurs rarely ask, "Is this going to work?" Instead, they are challenged by, "How can we make it work?"

COMFORT ZONE

We confine ourselves to comfortable limitations. It seems so much easier to do the familiar. Sometimes it is good to stretch our comfort zone and attempt what we may not feel *gifted* in.

Group brainstorming

At a meeting in a paint company, technicians were seeking new ideas for removing paint. One man humorously suggested mixing dynamite with the paint. That way, years later, they could toss a match at the painted wall and blow it off.

Once the laughter died down, the group took this bizarre idea and came up with a surprising solution: Mix a chemical with the paint that could react later with the paint if pasted over it to dissolve it. This is how paint remover was invented.

Is there any reason a group of Christians cannot excel in brainstorming? A stroke of genius is sometimes *modified stupidity*. Knowing this may help us break through inhibitions.

Summary

Creative thinking entails using our imagination for inventing original ideas to solve problems. Barriers exist in this process. Effective leaders overcome them.

From this chapter we learn

- God wants us to indulge in creative thinking because he gave us the faculty of imagination to do it.

- Numerous barriers to creative thinking exist. We need to be aware of them.

- Brainstorming is a good way to practice our creative faculties.

Study Questions for Chapter Eight

1. What is creative thinking?

2. Can you give an example of creative thinking from your own experience in a Christian context?

3. List some of the barriers to creative thinking.

4. What is brainstorming? Do you think it might work in your particular cultural context?

---

1. Isaac Asimov, the great science fiction novelist in a radio interview, said most people could write a story if they would concentrate on it hard enough. He claimed talent was secondary. A disposition to hard work was the secret.
I took this as a challenge because I felt he was underestimating the talent. So over a weekend I concentrated as hard as I could on a story idea. The result: A 6000 word story on my web site I titled, Phobia. It is a lousy example of science fiction but that is beside the point. Azimov was right.
2. Illustration taken from A Whack on the Side of the Head by Roger Von Oech, Ph.D

Chapter 9

Relationships Among Christian Leaders

Privileges and Ethics

In the first two chapters, we learned about servant attitudes and integrity along with a disposition to embrace suffering. There is another side to this coin.

According to Scripture, God's ordained leaders have certain rights and privileges no one may disregard without due process.

Our current culture tends toward independence, individualism and a distrust of institutions. These attitudes may cause a disregard of the spiritual authority God gives ministers. If church members submit to him, they may do so because they like him, not because they respect his office or acknowledge his spiritual authority.

———— ◄O► ————

GOD'S ORDAINED LEADERS HAVE
RIGHTS NO ONE MAY DISREGARD
WITHOUT DUE PROCESS

Worse, we as ordained ministers might inadvertently violate the rights of our fellow ministers. [1] We may end up treating our colleagues as less than what the Word of God says they are. If we understand the rights of ministers, we can avoid treating our fellow ministers unethically. Some of these rights and privileges are:

The right to respect

> *Let the elders who rule well is counted worthy of double honor, especially those who labor in the word and doctrine.* 1Timothy 5:17

The preaching and teaching of the Word is so central to Christian ministry, we must be careful to honor those called to it. This includes avoiding derogatory comments about a fellow minister.

There are exceptions, nevertheless. We have the right and mandate to speak against heretics whether they call themselves ministers or not. In fact, these are not fellow ministers. Romans 16:17,18

Disciplinary cases involving ministers is another exception. So is evaluating a fellow minister for consideration for future work. Negative evaluations may be correct in such a setting.

We treat fellow ministers as equals, because that is what they are before God. In reformed ecclesiology, there is no higher rank than the ordained minister. Some ministers have earned more respect than others because of their experience or accomplishments. But under no circumstance are we to treat any minister as less than a minister of Christ.

Conversely, this means ministers have a right to defend themselves against abuses from others, when necessary to do so for the honor of the gospel. This is the entire point behind 2Corinthians as well as 1Corinthians

Chapter Four. Paul had to defend against a disdainful attitude from the Corinthian believers. He did this not for his sake alone, but for the honor of the gospel and because their attitude was sinful.

Being a servant predisposed to suffering does not mean a leader must let himself be walked on. When the honor of the gospel is called into question, he not only has a right to defend himself, he has that obligation.

The right to one's own domain of ministry

> *...to preach the gospel in the regions beyond you, and not to boast in another man's sphere of accomplishment.* 2Corinthians 10:16

And so I have made it my aim to preach the gospel, not where Christ was named, lest I should build on another man's foundation, Romans 15:20

Even the Apostle Paul recognized the concept of "territory" in ministry. Every minister has his "sphere" that we respect. If a minister is working in a certain area, we avoid infringing. We refrain from building our church next door to another legitimate evangelical work. We avoid evangelizing villages where others are evangelizing. By the term *another man's foundation,* Paul recognized others have ownership of the ministries they found.

The right of authority over our own flock

> *Therefore take heed to yourselves and to all the flock, among which the Holy Spirit has made you overseers, to shepherd the church of God which He purchased with His own blood. (29) For I know this, that after my departure savage wolves will come in among you, not sparing the flock.* Acts 20:28

The Holy Spirit gives a particular flock to each minister to shepherd. From this we deduce certain ethical principles.

We do not steal sheep from another minister's flock. Some consider themselves and their denominations so superior they feel justified in taking people from other legitimate evangelical groups. This is a religious form of thievery.

Freedom from accusations without due process

> *Do not receive an accusation against an elder except from two or three witnesses. (20) those who are sinning rebuke in the presence of all, that the rest also may fear.* 1Timothy 5:19

The right to be judged by one's own peers

Due process means a hearing before one's ministerial peers by which a minister can answer accusations made against him. According to the above text, this right includes at least two things.

No congregation has the right to receive accusations against a minister. Timothy, not the congregation, had the authority to receive accusations against the elders. Even then, substantial eyewitness evidence is necessary.

The accused ministers have nothing to prove. All burden of proof is on the accusers. If they fail to substantiate their accusation, they have committed slander and must be rebuked.

The right of voice and vote in all matters concerning his ministry

We would think this is self-evident. It is astonishing how it is overlooked. [2]

A Christian hierarchy will usually treat its workers more like employees than fellow ministers. The rights and privileges the Bible guarantees ministers get washed overboard in the maelstrom of bureaucracy.

EXAMPLE: A mission board was writing its policy manual. They considered how to get a correct perspective of crisis situations on missionary teams. Believe it or not, they actually adopted the following policy: *"Perceptions of reality shall be those of the team leader."*

This absurd statement assumes the leader could never be the cause of the crisis, his perceptions will always be accurate and the other ordained ministers on the team may safely be disregarded. [3]

We see in several instances how even the Apostles avoided imposing authority over ordained elders. They recognized the right of others to be consulted in matters affecting them.

EXAMPLES:

At the Jerusalem council, Acts 15, all the elders present had voice and vote, even though they were not apostles.

To Philemon, Paul says: *But without your consent I wanted to do nothing, that your good deed might not be by compulsion, as it were, but voluntary.* Philemon 1:14

As an Apostle, Paul could have given orders. He didn't. Consistent with Christian leadership style, Paul refused to by-pass Philemon's domain of influence.

Regarding Apollos, Paul says: Now concerning our brother Apollos, I strongly urged him to come to you with the brethren, but he was quite unwilling to come at this time; 1Corinthians 16:12

Paul *urged* him but did not command him.

No one, regardless of their rank in a hierarchy, has a right to bypass an ordained minister by making decisions affecting that man's ministry without granting him voice in the matter. Doing so is discourteous and immoral.

The practice of parity: Tips for good relationships among ministers

THE PACT AMONG LEADERS

Two or more leaders can make an agreement among themselves to defend each other when one is verbally attacked, especially in his absence. This presents a united front, which tends to silence critics. They learn that if they want to verbally attack your colleagues, they had better do it outside of your hearing.

What if the critic is correct in his assertion? Tell him the other ministers or leaders are capable of dealing with the matter.

God may defend the leader even when the man is wrong in a decision. It seems God defends His own honor in such cases because He is the one who appointed the man. Leaders must beware of pride at this point. Some leaders assume a positive outcome is God's stamp of approval on their decisions. This can be self-deception. [4]

INTEGRITY, NOT CONTROL

I do not control other people nor allow others to control me. Is this attitude arrogant and independent? Not if integrity is the foundation of your relationships with those in authority over you. Control is one-way leaders might relate to people but it is not a godly one. The godly way is on another basis: Integrity.

KEEPING AGREEMENTS

When we give our word, we must keep it even if it is inconvenient. The psalmist says the man is blessed *"who keeps his oath even when it hurts."* (Psalm 15:4) We keep our promises because we are made in the image of God and He keeps His word.

Nothing is wrong with asking someone to renegotiate an agreement because of unforeseen factors. We do not, however, have the moral right to break it just because we may have the power or authority to do so.

WHEN WE GIVE OUR WORD, WE MUST KEEP IT EVEN IF IT IS INCONVENIENT

This is doubly true in relationships with ministerial colleagues. If you become a Christian leader in an influential organization, the temptation may be to break inconvenient agreements simply because you have the authority to get away with it. The power to do a thing and the right to do it, are different issues.

I have observed how powerful organizations may view agreements as unilateral, binding the weaker party only, allowing them to change it with immunity. This is simply another form of the arrogance we discussed in Chapter Three.

Beware of this tendency if you become a leader in an organization. If you make agreements, do your best to keep them. Otherwise, it will erode your integrity, which ultimately undermines your right to lead.

ACCOUNTABILITY GROUPS

Every leader needs to be accountable to somebody, whether the system he is in requires it or not. Pick out two, or at the most, three friends who will agree to be an accountability group for you. This means you will keep them advised of important issues affecting you and will listen their counsel.

> *...and in a multitude of counselors there is safety.* Proverbs 24:6 (KJV)

A group may simply exist as an advisory committee to give counsel when encountering difficulties in your ministry.

I have an advisory committee of this sort, consisting of a pastor and an elder. I formed this group a number of years ago while under attack from abusive leaders. Since I knew my emotional involvement might cloud my perception of reality, I chose two men to help me. These turned out to be more than helpful. They were indispensable in a tough situation I could not have handled on my own. They went to bat for me when it counted.

The two I chose for my personal accountability group are men of moral courage. They did not hesitate to fight for me when it counted when I was the party in the right. Finding them took a lot of searching because such men are rare.

Ask God to give you men of absolute integrity and moral courage to whom you may be accountable. He will give them. Just remember...chose carefully. Some guys talk a good fight.

The terms of my agreement with my personal committee are simple: I agreed to keep them advised of everything of importance that may seriously affect my ministry. This includes potential crisis situations as they may develop, along with any major changes in ministry. I agreed to make no important decisions against their counsel without very thorough consideration.

EVERY LEADER NEEDS TO BE ACCOUNTABLE TO SOMEBODY, WHETHER THE SYSTEM HE IS IN REQUIRES IT OR NOT

T IP: Be very careful to choose just the right men for such a committee. You want people with a certain indispensable quality: *Uncompromising moral courage.* Without this trait, your committee is worthless.

Summary

God's ordained leaders have certain rights and privileges. These include the right to respect, freedom from accusations without due process and authority over their own domain of ministry. If we understand these rights, we will be better prepared to avoid sinning against our colleagues by violating them. Creating their own private accountability or advisory committee helps keep them on track and ethically sound.

From this chapter we learn

- Those God appoints to leadership have certain scriptural rights and privileges. It is unethical to ignore these.

- Their spiritual authority and office must be respected, even though they are not always right.

- They have the right to voice and vote in all matters affecting their ministry.

- Another important right includes freedom from accusations without due process.

- It is advisable for every leader to be accountable. This is a safeguard.

Study Questions for Chapter Nine

1. What are the rights and privileges accorded by Scripture to God's appointed leaders?

2. Describe the rights and privileges the Word of God accords leaders.

3. Why is an accountability or advisory committee recommended?

4. What characteristics do you would like to see in leaders with whom you associate?

---

1. This is especially true if we work in a complex hierarchical structure, as described in Chapter Three.

2. It is always overlooked in complex hierarchical structures.

3. The name of this mission is withheld for reasons of discretion.

4. I once worked with an evangelist who did this constantly. His lack of administrative ability often created chaos. God, merciful as always, would bail him out and then he would say, "See? I was right all along." He nearly drove me nuts.

PART TWO: Practicalities

Chapter 10

Communicating With Subordinates

A common error in Christian leadership is poor communication. Many leaders commit typical communication mistakes that cause friction. We need to be aware of these.

ASSUMED COMPREHENSION

I once taught Spanish to eighth graders. On one occasion, I took forty-five minutes to explain how to conjugate a Spanish verb. At the end, I asked if there were any questions. A student raised his hand and asked, "Mr. Smalling, what is a verb?"

The class was wasted for that student and it was my fault. I assumed they all knew what was a verb and proceeded without giving them the necessary foundation.

As a leader, never *assume* your subordinate understands their job. Always *verify*. If misunderstanding occurs, it is *your* fault not theirs.

Imagine yourself working at a job, convinced you are doing it right. Along comes your supervisor and says, "What on earth are you doing? That's not the way to do that job!" Then he reprimands for not knowing how to do the job right.

Have you ever had such an experience? Most of us have. You assume you are doing your job right until a supervisor comes along and tells you it is all-wrong. Question: Who is at fault? Answer: The supervisor. It is his fault for not communicating. It is not your fault for not knowing.

———◆○◆———

As a leader, never assume your subordinate understands his job. Always verify.

———◆○◆———

THE INCOGNITO SYNDROME

There are people who carefully arrange their lives so it is nearly impossible to contact them. They never seem available. They avoid answering their phone, leaving the answering machine to do it. While their attitude is not hostile, one gets the impression of, "Don't call me. I'll call you at my convenience." People come into their lives when and if they decide.

Two things are notable about these personalities: First, they have no business being in Christian leadership. Second, they are frequently Christian leaders. We call these types, Mr. Incognitos.

A missionary team on which I served had a team leader who was just such a type. The team members all had their residences in the city. His was in the country. Every member had a telephone, except him. People complained about him being unavailable so he got a cell phone which in that country a lot of money to the team fund. It did not work much of the time.

After a while, we began to refer to him privately as "Mr. Incognito." The team mentally wrote him off and ignored him. Fortunately, most of the team were self-starters who needed little supervision. This syndrome created a leadership vacuum. He had lost his leadership and could not communicate enough to figure it out.

In contrast with Mr. Incognito, is the example of the pastor of a Presbyterian church. I needed to visit him on business one day. I went into the office and introduced myself to the secretary, explaining I wished to see the pastor. I apologized that I had not made an appointment. The secretary ignored this comment and said, "The pastor's office is just around the corner here. Go right in."

I paused and said, "Don't you need to announce me?" She said, "No. The door is open. Just go right in." Sure enough, the door was open and he was sitting behind a large desk, writing. I knocked on the door frame. He smiled and said, "Come in!"

He dismissed my apology for interrupting him and indicated he was attentive to me. He said, "There is nothing I do more important than people. People are my business. That is why I am here. It is not an interruption. I simply do other work between people."

Later I reflected, "I wonder if this pastor's attitude has anything to do with the fact that he has 2000 people in his church."

THE HOVERING HAWK SYNDROME

Have you ever had a supervisor who stands over you to watch everything you do? Did you feel comfortable? Did you perform better or worse?

Give subordinates room to breathe and avoid smothering their creativity.

If you give a job to someone, make sure they understand what is expected then leave them alone to do it. You can check in on them diplomatically with the question, "Do you need anything?"

Constant feedback is an important key to avoiding problems with your subordinates. Ask your people what they think about the job to be done. You will be amazed how often they totally misunderstood.

Do this however, without insulting their intelligence. Avoid the condescending statement, "I want you to repeat to me what I just said."

UNILATERAL DECISIONS WITHOUT CONSULTING

On a missionary team, one leader tended to make decisions without consulting the other ministers in his team. This caused his team to feel their opinions and persons were meaningless. The feeling of being disregarded and disdained tended to result in a counter reaction of the same kind. The team began to disregard and disrespect the leader.

Leaders who do this give the impression they consider themselves far wiser than those around them. Leaders may get so busy, they sometimes forget the importance of input from subordinates. They simply want to get things done expediently. Arrogance may not be the cause of these unilateral decisions. But to subordinates, it certainly looks like it.

Unilateral decisions are particularly damaging in Christian circles because everyone is a volunteer. People have a much lower tolerance for abuse when they are not obliged to be there.

People naturally tend to react in like kind to the way in which we treat them. If we show esteem the input of our subordinates, they are more likely to respect our decisions.

NEGATIVE-ONLY COMMUNICATION

Another type of leader communicates with his subordinates only when he is displeased. When he makes an appointment with someone, that person knows automatically he is displeased. Guess what stress this puts on the subordinate!

People learn to avoid him. They show him respect outwardly but in private they neither esteem his person nor heed his counsel.

Summary

Good communication is almost synonymous with good leadership. Leaders need to walk a line between too much supervision and too little. Subordinates cannot read our minds and it is our responsibility to make sure they understand what we expect of them.

From this chapter we learn

- Good communication with subordinates is essential to leadership.

- Some leaders assume their people understand what is expected of them when this may not be the case.

- Some leaders smother their subordinates with too much supervision.

- Unilateral decisions without consulting those involved may cause resentment and disrespect.

- Communicating only when something is wrong makes a leader less desirable to be around.

Study Questions for Chapter Ten

1. Give an example of how you would supervise a group of believers painting the interior of the church, taking into account a balance between supervising too much and supervising too little.

2. How can you involve people in the decision-making process without turning it into a democratic vote?

3. Think of a leader whom you know and admire. Describe this person's style of communication.

4. Think of a leader whom you know and do not admire. Describe what this person's style of communication.

Chapter 11

Communication: Positive affirmation

Why positive affirmation?

H ave you ever had a supervisor in the workplace who only communicated with you when he was correcting you for something wrong? How did you feel when he approached? "UH OH! Here he comes again! What did I do wrong this time?"

What kind of atmosphere did that produce in the workplace?

In their book, *One Minute Manager*, Blanchard and Johnson shows why the power to create an atmosphere in the workplace, whether positive or negative, is in the hands of the leader. The authors recommend that out of every ten communications with a subordinate, nine should be positive. This includes congratulating him for a job well done.

In the workplace, bosses seem to fear if they praise an employee, he might ask for a raise. [1] Even though this is not a factor in the church, the need for positive affirmation is even more acute. After all, people are not obliged to be there. Here are some reasons why praising our people, briefly and sincerely, is an essential part of communication.

Positive affirmation...

MAKES PEOPLE WANT TO LIVE UP TO YOUR EXPECTATIONS OF THEM

If they think you have a positive image of them, they will live up to it.

There is a tale about a man with a mutt named Fido. One day, the man got his pet a collar with his name, spelled *Phydeaux*. After that, when the man walked him down the street, the dog strutted with his head high. He was no longer a mutt. He was the neighborhood aristocrat.

Affirming someone in a specific and genuine manner will have them holding their head a little higher.

MAKES YOU A MORE APPROACHABLE PERSON

Remember, people will judge your value as a Christian leader more on the way you treat them personally than on the quality of your sermons, the accuracy of your decisions or administration of the church.

We often prefer a doctor more for the way he talks to us than the competency of their decisions. We have no training to judge medical treatment. So we tend to judge the doctor's competence more on social skills than anything else. This is irrational of course, but it is reality.

The same is true with your congregation. They have not been to seminary. They have not taken homiletics and do not know how a sermon is structured. Some may think "exegesis" refers to the exit sign on the door. They do know, however, how you treat them.

Below is a simple system for praising a person in just a few seconds. It is based on Blanchard's concepts, modified for Latin culture. [2] Practice this as a habit and you will be amazed what it does for your relationships.

The pattern

BE BRIEF

A congratulatory remark need take no more than a minute, usually less. If you elaborate more, it sounds phony. Approach the person in a casual manner.

BE SPECIFIC

Pick out a detail of the work accomplished and mention it. This shows the person you actually did notice the work done and is not just being polite.

EXPRESS HOW IT MAKES YOU FEEL

This shows you are vulnerable. The other party realizes they have power to affect you emotionally. This is essential for any normal relationship.

ENCOURAGE HIM TO CONTINUE

Even if the work done is not something he will repeat, you can encourage him to continue the same work ethic or good attitude.

EXAMPLE: You have asked Henry to arrange the chairs for the Sunday morning service because the deacon who normally does it is away. You instruct Henry how to do it. On Sunday morning when you go into the church early for the service, you notice Henry has just finished. Here's what you say:

> "Hi, Henry. You did a good job arranging the chairs. I noticed you put them about three inches apart so people would not feel crowded. That was thoughtful. It makes me feel good to know I have somebody I can rely on in a pinch. Keep up the good work."

Notice the elements:

- You were brief. This took no more than 20 seconds.

- You were specific. Chairs three inches apart.

- You mentioned how it made you feel. It made you feel good to have a reliable person to help.

This pattern is simple to learn and to practice. Try to do this with at least five people a week and eventually it will become a habit. You can do it with store clerks, service personnel or family members.

TIPS:

DO NOT FLATTER

It will come across as phony. Honest and clear communication is the only form that the Bible recognizes in leadership.

CONGRATULATE IMMEDIATELY

The sooner you speak to the person after the job is finished, the better. The effect is stronger.

DO THE CONGRATULATIONS BEFORE OTHER PEOPLE

This honors them before their peers. Such feedback is a powerful tool for motivating people.

TOUCH THE PERSON, OR SHAKE HANDS

This depends on culture or personal preference. Some people consider it an oversight if you do not.

AFFIRM THEM IN THEIR ABSENCE

This is really effective in relationships. "You know, Bill, I noticed Freddy did a really good job on the chairs. He seems a person we can rely on." You can be sure Henry will eventually hear about what you said.

Summary

Good communication is the responsibility of the leader, not the subordinate. He must ensure people understand what is expected and be verbally rewarded when they do it. Good leaders create a positive atmosphere by recognizing the accomplishments of others, simply and sincerely.

From this chapter we learn

- Never assume people understand what you expect of them. Verify it.

- Use positive affirmation to encourage people and create a positive atmosphere.

- Be sincere and honest in your communications, without flattery.

Study Questions for Chapter Eleven

1. Describe a couple of the common communication errors mentioned in this chapter.

2. Write out a sample congratulatory remark to a person, using the brief system described in this chapter.

3. By what criteria do people judge a leader?

4. Can you think of other ways to create a positive atmosphere in your church, other than those mentioned in this chapter?

5. Good communication is the responsibility of the leader, not his subordinates.

HOMEWORK: Congratulate five people this week, using the system in this chapter and write a brief description of each incident.

---

1. Blanchard claims research shows this to be untrue. People often work harder for approbation than for money. One Minute Manager. p.3
2. Blanchard, Kenneth. One Minute Manager. Berkley Publishing: Berkley, CA, 1984.

Chapter 12

Communication, corrections and reproaches

From time to time a leader must correct a follower. In daily life, this usually involves minor issues easily corrected, not serious moral conduct. Correcting others makes us nervous. We naturally dislike confrontations, preferring amiable relationships with everyone.

Are there ways to do this smoothly and more comfortably for both you and the other person? Yes. If you adopt a short, simple pattern for correcting, you will soon become more comfortable at it. Even better, your people will learn to recognize the pattern and feel more comfortable with your corrections.

The pattern for correction is the same as for praising...with a couple of minor differences. Let's go over the basic pattern with an example and then take a look at general tips on when to apply it.

Example: Freddy the liar

A new convert in the church, a young man named Freddy, has the habit of telling white lies. [1] You would like to help him but have not yet caught him in one.

Freddy misses church one Sunday. You learn from two members he was in the park playing football. During the week you see Freddy on the street and mention you missed him last Sunday. Freddy says, "My grandmother who lives in a nearby town was seriously ill. I went to visit her. That is why I was not in church."

You have just caught Freddy in a lie. How do you handle it?

The correction:

YOU: "Freddy, two of the members saw you playing football in the park on Sunday. You just lied to me, didn't you?"

FREDDY: (With head lowered.) "Yes. It was a very special game with the team I belong to and I did not want to let them down."

YOU: "I understand, Freddy. I'm not against football. You are new in Lord and I'm here to help you grow. Let me help you with something... Christians always tell the truth because lying is sin. This is true even of small lies like this one. It makes me feel really sad when a fellow Christian lies to me because that is not what Christians normally do. I know what damage it can do to your walk with the Lord. You need to ask God to forgive you for that."

(At this point you **pause**, look at him and wait for his reaction. I call this the *uncomfortable pause*. It gives impact to what is being said.)

FREDDY: "Yes, you're right. I shouldn't do that."

YOU: "I forgive you. I appreciate your walk with the Lord and commitment to the church. I am committed to helping you grow in the Lord. Feel free to call me any time you need help with anything." (Here, you shake hands.)

Notice the similarity in pattern with positive affirmation in the previous chapter:

YOU DID THE REPROACH IMMEDIATELY AFTER THE OFFENSE

If you wait until another occasion, you will give the impression you keep a mental list of the offenses of others. This will damage your relationship.

BRIEF

You avoided preaching a sermonette. A minor offense calls for brevity. The whole correction took no more than a minute. You are not interested in embarrassing him. You are interested in instructing him, so you get to the point immediately.

SPECIFIC

You did not call him a liar. You pointed out a specific lie and implied it is not something characteristic of him.

EXPLAIN HOW IT MAKES YOU FEEL

You mentioned how it makes you feel. This indicates you are a pastor not a judge. You are not in the least "objective" about the matter and have no intentions of being so. You are affected by what Freddy does. You are vulnerable. This is the kind of attitude people can relate to.

THE UNCOMFORTABLE PAUSE

This an element not included in the positive affirmation. It gives time for your reproach to have impact. It also allows the person to make a decision: Repent or not. If he chooses to repent, he will normally do so at that moment.

AFFIRMATION OF WORTH

You ended by forgiving him for lying to you. Then you reaffirmed your commitment to him and openness to help him in the future.

Some important things you did not do:

YOU DID NOT REPEAT YOURSELF

Leaders with a gift of preaching may be tempted to fall into this. Once you have done the reproach and he has repented, drop it. The only reason to elaborate is if he does not repent and instead makes excuses.

YOU DID NOT BRING UP OTHER INCIDENTS OF LYING YOU KNEW ABOUT

Have you ever had someone bring up a fault you committed months before? How does it make you feel? Inside, you are thinking, "Months have gone by and this guy has held this against me all this time and said nothing. I cannot trust this person."

You will do irreparable damage to your relationship with Freddy if you do this to him. You might *feel* like doing it in order to support your view that he is an habitual liar. This is a grave mistake.

YOU DID NOT CALL HIM A LIAR

You said he told a lie. The difference is between an habitual characteristic and an anomaly. Even if you know Freddy is an habitual liar, you cannot say it until you catch him in it habitually. Then you have a problem on a different level.

YOU DID NOT TRY TO FLATTER HIM BEFOREHAND

Have you ever had a person come up to you with a complimentary remark and then follow it up with a rebuke? How did you feel about this reproach? You probably felt manipulated. You may have felt "set up." Did you trust that person more afterwards, or less?

Do not "butter up" the person first. Get straight to the point. Avoid mixing positive affirmation with negative affirmation. Avoid flattery. People will perceive you as more honest.

Repeated offenses: The verbal contract

What if this is the third time you have caught Freddy in a lie? Now you can honestly say to Freddy that you detect he has a habit and you would like to help him with this area. A superb way to help is with the *Verbal Contract*. It goes something like this:

> **You**: "Freddy, this is the third time we have talked about this. I know you are growing in the Lord and doing better. I have an idea that could help you get completely free from this. We can work on this problem together. We'll meet once a week for a month. At that time I'll ask you how many times you lied during the week. You will tell me the truth. I won't criticize you or condemn you. We'll pray about the problem together. Talking about it will help you overcome it."

> If Freddy agrees to this, it will surprise him how quickly he overcomes the habit. Why? Accountability to someone is effective. If we know we will have to tell someone about it next week, we are more likely to resist the temptation.

Summary

People occasionally need correcting for minor offenses. Correcting is one of the uncomfortable duties in Christian leadership. Using a simple pattern helps alleviate the discomfort. If your honesty and openness to help people comes across, you will have more success.

From this chapter we learn

- Correcting people is part of a Christian leader's duty.

- A good procedure for doing the corrections helps alleviate the natural stress one feels in confronting people.

- We need to correct immediately after the offense.

- We need to be specific and clear, showing how the offense affects us and thus showing ourselves to be vulnerable.

- Avoid mixing positive with negative affirmation.

- If necessary, make a verbal agreement.

Study Questions for Chapter Twelve

1. Describe the pattern for correcting someone in a minor offense. Invent an incident in which you correct someone and write it out.

2. Why is it important to correct people immediately after an offense?

3. What are some possible errors a leader may commit in correcting people?

4. What is a *Verbal Contract* relative to correcting people and when it is necessary?

5. Explain the value of the *Uncomfortable Pause*.

---

1. As Christians we realize all lies are serious. We use this expression for convenience only.

Chapter 13

The Three Hammers

We can think of rebuking as a progressive process. I call them the three hammers: Rubber hammer, wooden hammer and steel hammer. The first time we correct a person with a serious moral problem, we do it with a certain degree of gentleness. (This is the rubber hammer.) If the person does not repent, we rebuke more firmly the next time. Each rebuke is sterner than the last.

People come in all shapes and sizes. So do their moral conditions. Some under your care may have annoying little habits like Freddy and his white lies. These may respond well to the little one minute corrections.

Others experience serious moral addictions like fornication, involvement with pornography or chemical addictions. These may require long-term counseling.

A category of moral issues that may indeed represent a serious danger is habitual gossip. Those who constantly criticize the leadership require stern correction.

A rebuke need not be loud or authoritarian. The first session may be along the lines of counseling. The second, with stern rebuke, etc. When people realize the next rebuke is likely to be more serious or result in discipline, they pay attention.

Gossips are especially dangerous. Leaders must be particularly alert to potential damage and be prepared to deal firmly with such people.

Rebuking is an act of love for God and for the person. The person receiving the rebuke may not think this is so at the time. Paul encountered this reaction with the Corinthians and we must be prepared for it.

REBUKING IS AN ACT OF LOVE FOR GOD AND FOR THE PERSON

Why? Because I do not love you? God knows I do! 2Corintians 11:11

The noetic effect

S in has a certain effect on the mind which theologians call the "noetic effect." [1] This term comes from the Greek work NOOS that means "mind," particularly that part of the mind having to do with perceptions of reality. [2] People in deep sin may be incapable of seeing their spiritual condition. [3]You as counselor must be prepared to confront this inability.

The Bible addresses this problem with terms like "blindness" and "hardness of heart."

To counter the noetic effect...

USE THE LAW OF GOD, THE TEN COMMANDMENTS, TO BRING CONVICTION

The Bible teaches that the Law is God's tool for revealing the seriousness of sin. Use it to remind the person of God's judgment on persistent sin and shallow repentance. Though Christians are not under the Law as a means of righteousness, nevertheless God will deal with serious sin in the life of a believer.

BE DIRECT AND CLEAR

Start your conversation with a serious tone, yet kind. In serious sin issues, we need not be so concerned about softening the blow.

REPEAT YOURSELF AT REGULAR INTERVALS

You will be surprised to discover they may not have processed what you said.

REQUIRE FEEDBACK

This is import to assure that he is tracking along with you.

BE CONSCIOUS OF TYPICAL REACTIONS FOR EVADING RESPONSIBILITY

See below on the many devices we humans use to avoid taking the blame for our actions.

FOCUS MORE ON WHY THE SIN IS AN OFFENSE TO GOD

I have observed that an aspect of the noetic effect is for the person to focus more on the earthly circumstances surrounding the sin rather than on how God views it. Some even focus on their own feelings.

This is especially true in sexual offense cases like adultery. Frequently the person will want to talk about how they felt about the person. Don't let them do this because they are only indulging in the same sin mentally rather than repenting of it. Make it clear their feelings about the act or the person are irrelevant. The issue is objective sin before God.

Getting through to a person under the noetic effect can be frustrating. It requires patience.

The Three Hammers

Therefore, rebuke them sharply, so that they will be sound in the faith. Titus 1:12 [4]

THE RUBBER HAMMER

Rubber is a relatively soft material. This represents the firm yet gentle rebuke. At all times we keep in mind the goal: Make them strong in the faith. Corrections are not vindictive.

THE WOODEN HAMMER

This rebuke is sterner. It could be accompanied with a warning of possible discipline.

THE STEEL HAMMER

After warnings, it may be necessary to resort to church discipline. [5]

Shallow repentance

What if the person *seems* repentant but you feel their repentance is shallow and insubstantial relative to the seriousness of the offense? A study on God's holiness sometimes helps if you can get them to do. You might recommend certain books for them to read. Among these are R.C. Sproul's HOLINESS OF GOD, A.W.Tozer's KNOWLEDGE OF THE HOLY and Stephen Charnock's section on God's holiness in EXISTENCE AND ATTRIBUTES OF GOD.

Possible signs of trivializing repentance

People who fail to repent immediately may show certain reactions to your counseling. Be aware of these:

COMPLAINING ABOUT THE COUNSELOR

Sometimes a person will say they are repentant when they are not. Genuine repentance is normally accompanied by contrition. The person will stop making excuses or blaming others or making light of their behavior.

How can we determine their level of repentance? Especially with sexual sin, the person may complain about the counselors. They say either they were not treated with love, or that the leadership did not follow proper procedure. If they do this, simply let them know these are signs of a lack of repentance and you will not listen to it.

GOING ELSEWHERE FOR COUNSELING

They do this to get the kind of counseling they want to hear. This is a form of self justification. Clarify that if they do this, you will consider it a form of rebellion. This will only add to their sin. Make it clear that God put them under the jurisdiction of the church and it is to the church they must submit. Otherwise they may be disciplined for contumacy.

It may be necessary to clarify this point to those church members who may be close friends. We have seen cases in which members or family have contradicted the counsel of the church leadership, thus creating further confusion.

There is a technique that sometimes works to prevent a person from seeking counsel outside the church. Warn him that a letter may be sent to any counselor he goes to. It will explain seeking counsel outside of church authority is an act of contumacy.

ATTEMPTING TO LEAVE THE CHURCH TO AVOID DISCIPLINE

Some churches have bylaws to deal with members who leave the church to escape discipline. The bylaws warn that a letter will be sent to any church he attempts to join, explaining the situation.

FOR THE REPENTANT

Pitfalls exist even for those you may successfully lead to repentance. Excessive remorse is rare, but it may happen. The case of the repentant incestuous man in 2 Corinthians 2 is an example. Paul was concerned he would be overcome with excessive sorrow.

Now instead, you ought to forgive and comfort him, so that he will not be overwhelmed by excessive sorrow. 2Corinthians 2:7

More often, a repentant person may tend toward legalism. Francis Schaeffer points this out in **True Spirituality**. A repentant believer must come into freedom from conscience and freedom in the thought life.
6

How to tell when a person, including yourself, is not truly repentant or is faking it

This is a general outline on techniques we all use to avoid repenting or for minimizing the seriousness of our sin.

Blame shifting

The other person did such and such and so I reacted accordingly. Or, I repent but the reason I sinned is because you did so and so to provoke me.

Blaming the circumstances

The circumstances caused me to do it. The fact of the case is that the only *cause* that God recognizes is our own sinful hearts.

Blaming one's own humanness

I'm only human. This really means, "God made me, so if I sin He is responsible. God is the sinner, not me."

Calling sin something else

Wrong choice: The fault is really and ultimately a lack of understanding on my part rather than a sinful heart.

Immaturity: The fault is a lack of growth, not my sinful heart. This actually blames *time* for our sin rather than ourselves. Time is not something that I control, therefore the blame is shifted to something that is not me and I am not therefore responsible.

MISFORTUNE: I *fell* into it. Sin was therefore like a hole in the ground I did not see, so I cannot be held responsible for it because I did not put it there. The reality is that was attracted to the hole in the first place because there was something in the hole my heart likes.

A TRIAL: Calling sinful conduct a trial rather than a sin. The Bible never does this.

SELF PITY: Acting like a victim of sin rather than a sinner.

TRIVIALIZING: The sin I committed is an isolated act non typical of what is in my heart. Or, the consequences are benign and therefore the sin is important. (All sin is important, although not all acts are equally sinful.) *My sin of gossip is not murder...therefore my sin of gossip is trivial.*

GENERALIZED CONFESSING: Asking forgiveness in vague terms for wrongdoing or sin in a very general sense. As in 'I'm sorry I offended you'; rather than 'I am sorry that I committed the sin of XYZ against you.'

What to do when a Christian *apologizes* to you in vague terms for offending you

Two questions to help both parties see the need of repentance:

- Exactly what sin did you commit that caused you to ask my forgiveness?

- Exactly what sin did I commit that provoked you to do that?

Observations in disciplinary situations [7]

Over several decades of ministry, I have observed certain dynamics entering into play when it becomes necessary to apply church discipline.

Counseling contains elements the leadership keeps discreetly within the boundaries of the counseling session. When it comes time to apply restrictions or discipline, the news will get out to the church members, but without all the facts. Some in the congregation may disagree with the discipline because they do not have all the details. They may think they do. This makes the leaders appear harsh.

In some churches, it is rare to apply discipline without losing a member, even if the offending party remains. What can be done about this?

The bad news: There is nothing you can do about it. You may try explaining to the church there are aspects of the problem the leadership cannot share. Some dissenting members will have the good sense to trust your judgment. Others will not. This is part of the burden of a Christian leader.

Leaders must learn to live with criticism. Sometimes it seems like a continuous background noise. [8]

The good news: In every situation I have observed in which the leadership has held their ground on godly discipline, and suffered loss as a result, God blesses the church above and beyond any losses. For every member who leaves offended, God sends others. He knows He can entrust His sheep to good hands.

Summary

Dealing with serious sin issues is not easy. The noetic effect may make it hard to get through to the offender about the seriousness of his sin. The leader must be firm but loving, persistent and patient. He may need to resort to progressively more stern rebukes according to the case. He must be able to assert his right to counsel and discipline if necessary. Doing so may incur reactions from those unfamiliar with all the facts. This is part of the cross the leader must bear.

God blesses faithful leaders who will not compromise their standards.

From this chapter we learn

- The noetic effect makes dealing with serious sin issues difficult.

-

Corrections need to be progressively firmer, as with the "three hammers."

- Sinning members may feign repentance, or the repentance may be shallow. A leader must be aware of signs of a lack of repentance.

- The church leadership may find it necessary to assert its right to exclusive counseling with the offender to avoid interference from others.

- The leaders may endure unjust criticism for the manner in which they deal with offenders.

Study Questions for Chapter Thirteen

1. What is the noetic effect?

2. What are the "Three Hammers" and what do they signify?

3. What are some of the signs of an unrepentant attitude on the part of a sinning Christian?

4. What are some of the stresses a leader may endure for faithfully applying church discipline?

5. What are some of the techniques you have used in the past to avoid repentance.

---

1. The Encyclopedia Britannica defines NOETIC as: "F. NOEIN to think. F. NOOS mind." Encyclopedia Britannica, Computer Edition, 2001 Search Criteria, "noetic."
2. "The faculty of perceiving and understanding." Thayer's Lexicon. Archa Publishers: Lafayette, IN, 1979 p. 429
3. An example of this usage by a theologian is John Frame, In Defense Of God's Creation. Internet site: http://www.theocentric.com/original articles/creation.html.

4. Paul was counseling Titus on rebuking Cretans. This culture apparently had a reputation for carnal behavior. Some cultures need sterner treatment than others. Others are less confrontive and we must be sensitive to the difference.

5. The subject of church discipline is for the Ecclesiology course. This chapter is more along the lines of counseling.

6. Schaeffer, Francis. True Spirituality. Tyndale Publishers: Wheaton, Il, 1971 p.83, 85

7. According to Scripture, churches must apply discipline to a member at times. This may involve rebuke, forbidding the Lord's Supper for that individual or even excommunication. (A detailed study on church discipline is the domain of a course on ecclesiology.)

8. Sanders brings out this point clearly in Spiritual Leadership, pp.121-126

Chapter 14

Dealing with Wolves

Keep watch over yourselves and all the flock of which the Holy Spirit has made you overseers. Be shepherds of the church of God, which he bought with his own blood. (29) I know that after I leave, savage wolves will come in among you and will not spare the flock. (30) Even from your own number men will arise and distort the truth in order to draw away disciples after them. (31) So be on your guard! Remember that for three years I never stopped warning each of you night and day with tears. Acts 20:28-31

A key function of the New Testament elder is to watch out for wolves that may destroy the flock. By wolves we mean false persons who may come in to provoke divisions and/or steal sheep.

Paul had to fight wolves constantly end we do too. He had his judiaizers. Today we have false Christians and false cults.

Two kinds of wolves

EXTERNAL

For I know this that after my departing shall grievous wolves enter in among you, not sparing the flock. Acts 20:29

Notice that they usually wait until the pastor or church planter is absent to enter in because they know that the overseer is likely to have discernment to spot them. The phrase "enter in" shows that they are from outside the fellowship. These are usually false cults and can be dealt with by warning the people in advance about which ones are current false cults: Jehovah's Witnesses, Mormons, Jesus Only, Church of Christ, etc.

These particular wolves are usually recognizable by name and are therefore not as dangerous as the other kind. Simple instruction to the converts about which groups to watch out for is usually sufficient. Note that Paul spoke about wolves as being a *certainty*.

INTERNAL

Also of your own selves shall men arise speaking perverse things to draw away disciples after them. Acts 20:30

These are the most dangerous kind, because they are good Christians gone bad and are already in the church. This kind is therefore the most difficult to detect and deal with.

These are often believers who have pride and ambition in their hearts (James 3:14-16), or dissatisfied for some reason. The devil begins to use them to draw away a following after themselves rather than after Christ.

Note: Both classes of wolves are self deceived and therefore do not see themselves as wolves.

Why does God allow wolves to come into the church?

For there must be also heresies among you, that they which are approved may be made manifest among you... 1Corinthians 11:19

At no time will you learn more about the people under your charge than when wolves come in. Their loyalties and stabilities will be put to the test. People that you thought were key people, may turn out not to be so. Others that you thought were weak will turn out to be stronger than you thought.

How to recognize wolves

THEY ALWAYS OPERATE BEHIND THE BACKS OF THE LEADERS: John 10:1,2

They will often visit the people in their homes without the permission of the church leaders. They will try to obtain authority or position in the church without going through the leaders. Jesus taught that they come disguised as God's sheep. Matthew 7:15-17

A key way to detect them is when they begin to steal sheep. Sheep don't steal sheep. Only wolves do.

THEY ARE CRITICAL OF THE LEADERS, USUALLY BEHIND THEIR BACKS: 2John 9,10

Everyone has weaknesses in his ministry, but this does not give people the right to go cutting them down with criticisms. The difficult lies at times in the fact that some of the things that a wolf may say may be true. But this is not justification for undermining the ministry of a person by criticisms, especially to weaker members in the church. Note some things that wolves said about Paul. 2Corinthians 10:10

THEY BOAST OF THEIR OWN SPIRITUALITY: 2Corinthians 10:12

Note here how Paul sarcastically mocks the spiritual pride of the wolves. They are often comparing themselves with others and the comparisons always seem to turn out in their favor. They frequently claim to have more light on some things than the missionary and may imply that they have more to teach than the missionary. 2Thessalonians 3:6

THEY TEND TO PROVOKE DIVISIONS: Romans 16:17,18

They invariably seek out the weaker believers. Romans 16:18 Wolves seem to have internal radar by which they seem to detect the believer. It may be a satanic form of discernment. They will invariably do directly to the weak believer and try to get in their favor.

How to deal with wolves

A man that is an heretic after the first and second admonition reject. Titus 3:10

Rebuking and rejecting

With nearly any other kind of problem with people, you normally demonstrate patience, compassion and mercy, but not so with wolves. You must show no patience, compassion, or mercy. Paul's instructions are clear: a wolf does not deserve more than two rebukes before throwing them out. Be very firm with them.

Example: A cultist comes into your church. He sits quietly and makes no disturbance but after the meeting sidles over to some weak believers. You discover he is getting addresses. You take him aside and warn him. He comes back again another time and does the same. Again, you warn him and make it clear that one more offense and you will have to close the door to him. Again he ignores you.

You then tell him to leave and not come back. A warning from the pulpit to the people may be necessary

Running interference

The whole church, especially the mature believers should be trained in how to run interference when a wolf enters.

This means simply intercepting the wolf before he or she has an opportunity to get to the weaker ones after the meeting, and engage them in conversation so that they will not have opportunity to do damage. All mature believers in the church should understand that they could be called upon to do interception duty if necessary.

From this chapter we learn

- An important function of an elder, according to the Bible, is to protect the flock from heretical and divisive people. The Bible uses the term "wolves" to describe this kind of person.

- Two kinds of wolves ambush the flock: The internal kind consisting of church members and the external kind, false cults. The most dangerous are the internal kind.

- It is essential to prepare mature members of the congregation to be ready to run interference against wolves from the outside.

Study Questions for Chapter Fourteen

1. What are the two kinds of wolves?

2. Describe at least three signs that a visitor may be a wolf.

3. How should you deal with a member of a false cult who attends your church.

Chapter 15

Divisive People

Heretics and rebels are divisive people who represent serious dangers to the church. The potential damage is enough to merit a study on its own. We deal with problematic people somewhat differently from those with other sorts of problems.

The book **ANTAGONISTS IN THE CHURCH** by Kenneth Haughk inspires much of the material in this chapter. This book is a must for any church leader. Some churches require it as reading for their church officers.

Other parts of this chapter are taken from my personal experience and that of fellow missionaries and ministries around the world.

Motivations

Problematic people are motivated by a desire for control. They cause division and confusion through complaining, criticism and resistance to authority. [1] Behind these symptoms is a drive for power. *Never* give it to them.

Characteristics in common

These characteristics need to be taken as whole. Not all will apply to one given individual.

- Incredibly tenacious

- Extremely high self-esteem.

- Aggressive

- Tendency toward anger

- Rigid attitudes

- Very manipulative and charming.

- Independent attitudes.

- Frequently very intelligent.

Antagonistic people rarely consider themselves the source of problems. Everyone else is the cause. Invariably, they consider themselves more insightful than those around them. They think if only they can get everyone to "see" their view, all will be wonderful.

The first signs of a pending problem with such a person are persistent complaining.

Antagonists will be critical of the condition of the church, especially the leadership. They will seek support for their views among the congregation. They may meddle in church affairs that are none of their business.

Dealing with antagonists

> *Warn a divisive person once, and then warn him a second time. After that, have nothing to do with him.* [2] Titus 3:10

GIVE THEM NO MORE THAN TWO WARNINGS

These people represent more danger to the church than any other type of problem. They can tear a church apart in short order. The sympathy and patience a leader normally demonstrates toward members with other types of sin, is inappropriate here.

Paul's commands in Titus 3:10 are not mere suggestions. Nor did he say, "counsel" them. He said to *"warn"* them. [3] Give the person *no more than two warnings.*

You cannot afford to play their game. This may seem compassionless. We must keep in mind that our primary compassion is for the flock God has put under our care and protection.

AVOID REASONING WITH THEM

Have you ever tried to reason with someone who considers you a fool? Did it work?

DON'T PLACATE THEM

Antagonists may consider kindness a form of weakness or fear.

DON'T GIVE THEM AUTHORITY OR RECOGNITION

Doing this is like trying to drown a fire with gasoline. They will use any authority or recognition as a platform to grab for more.

AVOID LENGTHY SESSIONS LISTENING TO THEIR COMPLAINTS

Problematic people will waste your time. In their mind, you need convincing why they are completely right. They will take up as much time as you allow, in order to make you see how right they are.

First meeting with the antagonist

In his book, Haughk gives practical suggestions on dealing with antagonists in two successive encounters. Some of the author's key suggestions are:

CHOOSE THE PLACE AND THE TIME

Do not let them choose it. [4] The meeting should be brief. It should not be over a meal or in a family atmosphere. State the amount of time you can give to them and stick to it. Doing this shows you are a person of your word. Haughk suggests no more than 20 minutes for the first session.

SAY AS LITTLE AS POSSIBLE

Let them do the talking. Hostile people may take anything you say, however innocuous, and use it as ammunition against you. They may quote you out of context.

TAKE PERSONAL NOTES

Report the facts to the other leaders in the church

DO NOT LET THE ANTAGONIST PUT YOU ON THE DEFENSIVE

Remember, you are not accountable to them. Your accountability is to God and your fellow leaders. Avoid the tendency to explain your actions. Maintain a professional attitude.

DO NOT ARGUE WITH THEM

You will not change their mind and will only provoke them

CLARIFY THEY WILL NEVER BE ALLOWED CONTROL

You can do this in a discrete way, not directly. When they see they will never have control, they may leave on their own accord.

FORBID THEM TO DISCUSS THEIR CONCERNS WITH OTHERS IN THE CHURCH

Make it clear you will not tolerate appeals to the congregation. If they do so, you will consider it an act of rebellion meriting discipline. If they cannot agree with the decisions of the leadership, it would be better to look for another church.

Second meeting with the antagonist

Suppose the antagonist has continued his divisive actions and ignored your instructions in the first meeting. The second and final meeting should be with the other church leaders present.

In this meeting the leaders should establish limits on the activities of the problematic person. They must warn them if they cross the boundaries, they may be excommunicated for divisiveness. Clarify this second warning is the final one.

Prevention: Teach your congregation

Haughk recommends the church teach its members how the leadership deals with problematic or discontent members. Show them the signs of the problematic person and teach them how to resist their influence. Make a *covenant* with the congregation, between them and the leadership, to work together to prevent this sort of thing. [5]

Summary

The church may come under attack from time to time by antagonistic or divisive people from within. The leadership needs a plan for dealing with such people. The temptation for some leaders is to use too much patience and compassion, ignoring Paul's injunctions in Titus 3:10. Church members need to be instructed in the seriousness of these problems and how to cooperate with leadership in dealing with them.

From this chapter we learn

- Divisive people have certain traits. Wise leaders are alert to them.

- Leaders need to know general principles in dealing with antagonists. This includes no more than two warnings, giving them no authority or control and showing at all times you, not they, are in control.

- The church needs to be taught how to cooperate with the leadership when attacks come from antagonistic people.

Study Questions for Chapter Fifteen

1. What are some of the key traits of antagonists or divisive people?

2. Explain why we should not be patient and tolerant with antagonistic or divisive people. Justify your answer from scripture.

3. Explain general procedures in your first meeting with an antagonist.

4. Explain general procedures in your second meeting with an antagonist.

---

1. From Antagonists in the Church by Haughk. Much of this chapter contains ideas found in this book, which is a MUST for any church leader.
2. The Greek term for divisive in this verse, HERETIKOS, may also mean one who follows a false doctrine. Thayer's Lexicon. Archa Publishers: Lafayette, IN, 1979 p.132
3. The Greek term NOUTHESIA may also mean "admonish." Louw and Nida, No. 33.321
4. Haughk even suggests that if the time and place they propose is convenient, you should nevertheless change it to send the message that you are the one in control.
5. Haughk has good advice about how to go about this with the church membership. The book is highly recommended reading.

Chapter 16

Minor Conflict Resolution and Diplomacy

This chapter deals with the leader's role as mediator in conflicts between two parties in a church setting. Serious and damaging dissention may occur in a church from time to time. On a daily basis, however, the leader is likely to encounter minor problems that these techniques can resolve. The extent of this book does not include analysis of more serious conflicts.

Assumptions

In the above scenario, the leader is not one of the parties in conflict. He is playing the role of mediator between two factions. The conflict is relatively minor, between people who know each other, involving questions such as how to proceed in a project, etc. Emotions and ego have entered into the picture.

Sometimes the leader is the last to know when a conflict is emerging in the church. People may hide contentions, fearing the leader may not take their side, hoping to resolve it themselves.

How do you know when a conflict is brewing?

A leader needs to be alert for typical symptoms of a pending crisis or conflict. One sign alone may not be a clear indication. Yet it should prompt a leader's attention to look for other symptoms.

CLIQUES

Certain people seem to make a point of avoiding each other. A small group of people making friends and bonding may be healthy. When two or more groups form like this around persons who seem to dislike one another, it is likely an underlying conflict is brewing.

ABSENTEEISM

When people are looking for another church, they may begin to attend irregularly. If they are doing this, it might be a good idea to find out what there is about the church they do not like. If their answers are vague, you may be uncovering a conflict situation with other people.

SILENCE

Some people stop communicating and isolate themselves when they feel in conflict. You might have to investigate to get the problem out into the open.

SARCASM

This is symptomatic of malice. It should be dealt with as malice, not as mere comments. Doing this requires a bit of probing.

FAILED WORK PROJECTS

Sometimes projects fail because they were lousy ideas in the first place. Frequently they fail because the wrong people were doing the work. Sometimes however, it is because the team was in conflict.

When should you intervene as a mediator?

Just because you are the leader does not necessarily mean you are the best choice for mediating the conflict. If one of the parties feels you favor the other, he may resist your mediation.

Though your office as leader gives you the legal right to be involved, it is more effective to obtain their agreement to do so. It is usually better to approach them as a servant offering to help, rather than as an authority figure bringing order.

You intervene when

- One of the parties asks you to mediate in the conflict.

- The effectiveness of a work group is hindered by the conflict.

- Both parties respect you.

Procedures during the meeting

Before anything else, pray for God's guidance.

CLARIFY TO THE PARTIES IN DISPUTE HOW THE CONFLICT IS AFFECTING EVERYONE

This helps change the focus from feelings to the facts of the case. People are generally more interested in their feelings than any other factor. As soon as they see how their conflicts are affecting the church or the project, you will have earned the *right* to intervene. Let them know why this conflict must be resolved.

ESTABLISH A MEETING TO RESOLVE THE CONFLICT

Explain, "This is a problem we three are going to resolve together." Clarify you are not a judge. You are there to help get the work back on track and you are not interested in mutual accusations. You are looking for a win-win situation.

ESTABLISH RULES OF PROCEDURE

Make it clear you are in charge of the meeting. The rules you establish depend on the situation. You might set rules, such as, when one person speaks the other will not interrupt. Or, that the participants must address their comments to you only, not to one another.

EACH PERSON SHOULD PRESENT HIS VIEW OBJECTIVELY

They should not attack each other and be specific, not general. Try to get them to present their views as though they were a third-party observer. The idea is to keep emotion out of it as much as possible.

ASK EACH PERSON TO GENERATE POSSIBLE SOLUTIONS

If the situation is emotionally charged you can ask the parties to *write out* their solutions on the spot instead of expressing them verbally. Compare them with your own. Afterwards you can express those resolutions they have in common. This forms the basis for the resolution of the conflict.

ASK EACH PERSON TO COMMIT TO THE RESOLUTION OF THE PROBLEM

Once you have come to agreement, make sure each party is committed to it. If one of the parties shows reluctance, you have accomplished nothing so far. Another meeting may be necessary. Or, you may simply have to make the decision for them.

General diplomacy techniques

Below are some techniques professional business negotiators use to resolve disputes. Sometimes these serve merely to gain better cooperation with people in situations not necessarily conflictive. These work in most benign situation, including between children in the home. [1] We can call these "win-win" techniques. [2]

TRIPLE OPTION PLAY

Instead of a simple choice between doing or not doing a thing, give a person several options and allow them to choose the one they think is better. Example: Do *not* say, "Would you like to help on repairs of the church this Saturday?" This requires a yes-no answer. It's easy for the person to simply say *no*. Instead, put it this way: "With which of these three areas do you feel most comfortable helping this Saturday, painting, washing windows or repairing furniture?"

CUTTING THE CAKE

Two children want the same piece of cake. The solution is to have one child cut the cake and the other child chose the first piece. The first child is motivated to divide the cake as evenly as possible. This may work for adults in dividing responsibilities or privileges.

HOLIER THAN THOU

Joe and Bill cannot come to agreement regarding responsibilities in the church. Ask them to write down what each thinks is the most equitable plan. Let them know you will submit these to a neutral party to decide which plan is most viable. It is remarkable how this technique brings agreement. Frequently the plans are nearly identical. This happens because it focuses on the task rather than rights.

SUBSTITUTION

Due to a mix up, both John and Bill were scheduled to do the announcements next Sunday. One of them will be put aside. How do you handle this diplomatically? Tell one of them you have a job for him, such as taking up the offering, equally important to the announcements.

TOSSING A COIN

The idea of casting lots to determine who gets which share of the inheritance is found in the Bible in Psalm 16:6.

TEMPORARY MEASURES

Let's try this for a month and see how it works.

GIVE ME A HAND

Instead of assigning a job, ask the person to *help* you. Do not say, "I want you to arrange the chairs next Sunday." The person may be thinking, "I do not care what he wants." It is better to say, "Can you help me with a problem? I will not be able to arrange the seats next week and I need someone I can rely on to do it. Will you be able to do this for me?"

THE REAL NEED

Sometimes people hide their real motives when complaining. A person may argue a point when all they want is a little appreciation. Sometimes you can find a way to meet this need in a way that is different from what they are asking.

From this chapter we learn

- A leader needs to be alert for signs of potential conflict brewing in the church. Signs could include cliques, absenteeism, silence, sarcasm or failed work projects.

- When conflict is detected, a leader must evaluate if he is the right person to resolve it.

- Negotiation techniques sometimes help to provoke a win-win situation.

Study Questions for Chapter Sixteen

1. What are some clues a conflict may exist among members?

2. How can you determine if you are the right person to resolve the conflict?

3. What are some good procedures during the meeting?

4. Describe briefly the following negotiation techniques:

   ○ Triple Option Play

   ○ Cut The Cake

   ○ Holier Than Thou

   ○ Substitution

   ○ Flip A Coin

○ Temporary Measures

---

1. For situations that are not benign, such as negotiating with difficult or stubborn people, Fry's Getting to Yes is the best book available. If people feel they are in competition with you and must "win" at any cost, this makes negotiating nearly impossible. Fry backs up a step and works on how to get them out of the competitive mode into working with you to solve a common problem.

2. In their book, The Power of Nice, Janowski and Shapiro make the adroit comment, "People who fight fire with fire usually end up with ashes." p.15.

Chapter 17

Decision Making

The leader is often called upon to make decisions that affect many others. It would be convenient if God would speak with an audible voice to those in leadership so we could be sure of our decisions. It is often a choice between two reasonable options. Sometimes we feel as though we are flying through a snowstorm.

If it were always clear what Christians or a church body should do, we would not need leaders. Making decisions when there is serious risk of making the wrong one is what Christian leadership is all about.

Decision making in leadership depends more on our personal devotional life than any other factor. A strong devotional life is central to the Christian leader because many are affected be his decisions.

DECISION MAKING IN LEADERSHIP DEPENDS MORE ON OUR PERSONAL DEVOTIONAL LIFE THAN ANY OTHER FACTOR

The reasoning process

R esearch is involved in making a decision. It is like the logic a detective uses to solve a crime.

A good detective starts out with no bias. He doesn't go about to prove anyone guilty or innocent. He does not say, "I don't like John. I'm going to prove he did it." He simply gathers clues to see where they lead.

Likewise, leaders must be careful to gather as much relevant information as possible. [1]

Sources of information

Often the evidence for the right decision will be a mixture of the spiritual and the material.

PERSONAL QUIET TIME

A leader should keep a spiritual journal, a notebook of what God seems to be teaching him through the Word. Divine guidance may come through this means.

In a church situation, God will normally have already indicated His will to some of the other leaders about the situation through the Word. Leaders should take seriously such coincidental evidence.

Prayer and fasting for seeking God on important decisions is biblical. Choosing leaders for service is one of those times.

> *While they were worshiping the Lord and fasting, the Holy Spirit said, Set apart for me Barnabas and Saul for the work to which I have called them. (3) So after they had fasted and prayed, they placed their hands on them and sent them off.* Acts 13:2,3

THE FACTS OF THE CASE, ALONG WITH LOGIC

God gave us brains and He expects us to use them. If the facts of the case seem to merit a certain decision, we generally go with the facts *after consulting with the Lord.* This means praying about it and checking to see if there are any godly principles being violated.

The Israelites in Joshua Chapter 9 learned the hard way to consult the Lord about everything. The Gibeonites invented a ruse to get Joshua and company to make an agreement with them. They claimed to have come from a very far country and showed old bread and worn out sandals to prove it. Everything looked perfectly logical. What does the text say? Joshua and his men fell into the trap. Why?

> *The men of Israel sampled their provisions but did not inquire of the LORD.* Joshua 9:14

Nevertheless avoid using only human reasoning in making decisions. Do not permit your leaders' meeting to degenerate into mere business meetings, as though it were a local corporation. [2]

COUNSELORS

> *...but in the multitude of counselors there is safety.* Proverbs 11:14 (KJV)

At times we do not have the luxury of consulting with our ministerial peers. However, when we do, we should take advantage of the wisdom of our colleagues.

THE INCUBATION PROCESS

God created us with a subconscious. This is a subliminal part of our brain that functions on its own. It has its own type of logic of which we are not usually conscious. If we encounter a complex and serious problem, we can allow our subconscious to work by a process we can call 'incubation'. We simply put in our minds all the relevant data and then do something else. Frequently the answer will come to our mind some time later.

This is a process that scientists use for *inspiration* in research. A famous historical example is the Greek philosopher Archimedes who found the answer to a difficult math problem while taking a bath. He had given up temporarily on the problem. During the relaxation of the bath, he noticed the displacement of water by his body. The answer was suddenly clear. "Eureka!" he shouted, ("I have found it!") His subconscious had been working on the problem in the relaxation of the bath.

There is nothing mystical about the incubation process. It is a perfectly natural phenomenon. Our brains are little computers. If we give our brains enough data, along with enough time, it will make associations we might have missed at first.

Summary

Making decisions as a leader can be a stressful process because we may not always be sure about the right course to take. The welfare of other people may be at stake.

Decision making is essentially the same as personal guidance from God. The difference is the leader is making decisions that affect the lives of more than just himself. This is why the leader's devotional life is essential.

Nevertheless, decision making is not a mystical process. Ordinarily it is a mixture of the subjective and objective...what the leader believes God is showing him through the Word and the Spirit at the time, along with the facts of the case.

From this chapter we learn

- Making decisions as a leader may seem risky because sometimes we are faced with several viable options.

- The wise leader gathers all the evidence he can about the matter before making decisions, avoiding preconceived ideas.

- Decision making for the leader is intimately connected with his personal walk with God.

- Forming decisions is often based on a combination of the spiritual with the material...the subjective with the objective. We use logic to make decisions but we depend on God to direct us.

- If time permits, we can let our minds process the facts of the case. Sometimes this will allow us to see options we had overlooked before.

Study Questions for Chapter Seventeen

1. Why is decision making in leadership sometimes stressful?

2. What is the role of the personal devotional life of a leader when it comes to making decisions?

3. Describe the process of reasoning by which a leader makes decisions. What are the sources of evidence a leader uses for making decisions?

4. What is the incubation principle?

5. What is meant by "the multitude of counselors"?

---

1. Scientists recognize this as the "Inductive" method of reasoning.
2. This is one reason to be careful not to overload your church board with businessmen. See Leadership Manual, Part One.

Chapter 18

Verbal Self-Defense

Circumstances may occur when it is legitimate for the leader to defend himself against unjustified verbal attacks. For the most part, we pay no attention unless criticisms come from the united voice of our ministerial colleagues. Sheep do not correct pastors.

When is self-defense legitimate?

VERBAL SELF-DEFENSE IS LEGITIMATE WHEN THE TRUTHS YOU PREACH ARE ATTACKED

Throughout the book of Galatians, Paul defended the gospel he preached as the only true one. His teachings against justification by law had been called into question. He defends himself by explaining he presented his teachings to the Apostles for validation.

> I went in response to a revelation and set before them the gospel that I preach among the Gentiles. But I did this privately to those who seemed to be leaders, Galatians 2:2

He then is able to start his epistle with Galatians 1:2 "... and all the brothers with me," This proved his gospel to be the right one. He defends his teaching when it is called into question. [1]

YOU MAY DEFEND YOURSELF WHEN THE LEGITIMACY OF YOUR CALL OR OFFICE IS PUT IN DOUBT

The Epistles of First and Second Corinthians clearly show the Apostle Paul defending his calling.

> *I care very little if I am judged by you or by any human court; indeed, I do not even judge myself.* 1Corinthians 4:3

Paul handles this criticism by declaring his critics to be inadequate judges. He tells them so in plain language. There may be times when you must do the same.

Within each church there should exist responsible entities such as a board of elders for determining if your ministry is meeting biblical standards.

If people in the congregation have complaints, they can present them in writing, with evidence, to the appropriate body. However, those who lodge ungrounded complaints may subject themselves to discipline as slanderers.

Dealing with habitual critics: Verbal judo

For several of these methods, we can thank Susanne Elgin's The Gentle Art of Verbal Self-Defense. This book is a recommended for a leader's library. [2]

Each church seems to have its self-appointed analysts and critics. Some have sharp minds by which they can dissect the church, your preaching and everyone else. Others may have personal problems and take them out on the pastor or other leaders. Sometimes we can use a little verbal judo [3] and deviate the attack harmlessly.

These techniques are intended for dealing with habitual complainers. (This assumes the criticism is unjustified.)

Underlying principles of verbal self-defense

NEVER REPLY TO THE ATTACK ON YOUR PERSON

Divert it to the *issue.* The intent of the attack is always to get you to defend your own person. Don't fall into this trap. Remember: You have no moral obligation to defend your ministry. According to 1 Timothy 5, the leader is never obliged to prove his innocence. The burden of proof is always on the accuser.

DIVERT THE ATTACK

You can return the attack back to the other person by asking questions that divert attention from your person to the theme in question, or to something abstract.

Techniques

Below, is the basic outline of the technique, followed by a good example of how to use it. Then we will illustrate the wrong way to deal with the attack.

TIME TRAVEL TECHNIQUE

Example one

Attack: Why do you always preach about condemnation?

Defense: "Since when did you first begin to imagine that I ....."

The right way to reply:

Attack: "Why do you always preach about condemnation?"

Defense: "Since when did you first begin to imagine that I preach excessively on condemnation?"

The wrong was to reply:

Attack: "Why do you always preach about condemnation?

Defense: (*Wrong* approach) "I *don't* always preach on condemnation! I preached on grace last Sunday. I don't think that my emphasis on condemnation is excessive, etc."

It is a mistake to argue whether you preach excessively on condemnation. This puts you on the defense. You turn the tables by focusing on an event in the past, rather than his attack on you. Instead, you question the validity of the critic's perception. This insinuates the problem is *really* located in the imagination of the critic rather than in your preaching. [4]

Example two

This attack is identical to the one above. Only the form of expression changes.

Attack: "Doesn't it matter to you that...?"

Defense: "Since when did you first begin to imagine that it does not matter to me?"

Attack: "Doesn't the condition of the Sunday school matter to you?"

Defense: "When did you first begin to imagine that the Sunday school does not matter to me?

Computer Technique

This technique involves acting emotionally detached. Computers are impersonal because they have no emotions. In this technique, you act as though you did not realize you are under attack. Instead, you speak as though the critic were referring to some abstract concept in which you are not personally involved.

Do not respond defensively to the attack on your person. Speak to the situation as though it were an objective and impersonal question having nothing to do with you.

The right way to reply:

Attack: "Since we have the new church board, the church has not grown."

Defense: "Church growth is an interesting science. The difference between the city and the country and between social classes makes it a complex question. Have you read a book on church growth lately?"

This defense turns the tables on the person. It deviates his comments as an abstract problem, not a personal attack on you. Second, you may reveal his ignorance if he has not studied the question. [5]

The wrong way to reply:

Attack: "Since we have the new church board which you organized, the church has not grown."

Defense: "Are you saying the board is incompetent or that I put it together wrong? I think the board is doing a good job...etc."

The attack insinuates you were wrong in the way you organized the church board and that both you and the board are incompetent. If you address that point, you fall into the trap. The person could claim they never actually said that and you are accusing them falsely. Since it was implied, not said, you find yourself in a dispute over whether they have attacked you and the board personally.

If you allow this, they win. Their whole strategy was to accuse you and the board before others without standing accountable for it. It doesn't really matter to them if you win the argument over what they *really* meant. They may even "apologize" for giving that impression. Nevertheless, the impression has already been given and that is exactly the intention.

This kind of attack is usually in a public setting because you are not really their audience. If the person has said this to you in private, you may want to sit down with them and discuss their feelings. [6]

Other techniques exist. These illustrate the basic principles for dealing with verbal abusers.

Summary

A leader may defend himself verbally if the value of his call or the truth of his teaching is assailed. Each ministry seems to have its self-ordained critics. Using tact and at times verbal judo, can help deflect the attacks harmlessly.

From this chapter we learn

- Verbal self-defense is sometimes justified.

- We can sometimes deflect groundless criticism with a little tact and technique.

Study Questions for Chapter Eighteen

1. When is it legitimate to defend oneself?

1. What are the basic principles of verbal self-defense?

---

1. Notice his appeal is to the body of ordained elders who have approved his ministry. His appeal is not to a congregational vote.
2. This book is helpful for many of life's situations, not just a church context.
3. In judo, one takes the attack and deviates it, turning the aggression against the verbal assailant.
4. Again, we are assuming the falsity of the accusation along with the lack of authority of the critic to make such accusations.
5. On the other hand, if he can speak knowledgeably about the subject, maybe you should listen to him. Remember: We are assuming here that the attacker is unduly critical.
6. We are still assuming here that we are dealing with an habitual critic rather than an ordinary church member concerned about the state of the church.

PART THREE: The Mentor

Chapter 19

The Heart of Mentoring

G reat news! Leadership training is simple.

I did not say *easy*. The core concept is simple. People are complex, each with his personality and sins.

In Chapter One we discovered there is only one Christian philosophy of leadership.... servant leadership, willing to suffer for followers and serve them with the dignity due God's image.

———◆———

THERE IS ONE BIBLICAL METHOD FOR TRAINING LEADERS: MENTORING

———◆———

J ust as there is one biblical philosophy of Christian leadership, so there is one biblical perspective of leadership training: *Mentoring*.

What is mentoring?

Mentoring is relational

Mentoring is a process involving a relationship between a leader and one being prepared for leadership.

This word incorporates abstract concepts, all revolving around relationships. Though the word "mentor" is absent from scripture, the Bible portrays it throughout.

This relational process shows up in Moses and Joshua, Elijah and Elisha, Christ and his disciples, Paul and Timothy and between Timothy and his elder candidates.

Mentoring is holistic

Mentoring for leadership encompasses the whole man...body, soul and mind. Academic disciplines are important, but not priority. Relationships take precedence in a specific order; with God, then man.

Christ, for example, was more concerned about the relationship of his disciples with him as Lord than their performance in the ministry or whether they understood the Law of Moses. Without this relationship, we are lawbreakers anyway, even if we have kept the letter of the Law, because we have broken the spirit of it.

This is why in our Visión R.E.A.L training system, the devotional life course comes first. It's about our relationship with God. The leadership course is second...our relationship with others.

We hear this approach in Paul's exhortations to Timothy, a young pastor. Paul considered every aspect of Timothy's life to have a bearing on leadership and therefore he addressed each area of Timothy's life.

Paul even expressed concern for Timothy's health and gave counsel regarding it.

For physical training is of some value, but godliness has value for all things,... 1Timothy 4:8

Paul's training of Timothy reflected nothing of the compartmentalized thinking in current western culture. Today, some may consider such procedure intrusive. Paul assumed it was natural to counsel Timothy in these private areas. His love and concern for Timothy made it possible.

THE INTELLECT IS IMPORTANT

Does mentoring replace academic preparation? In no way!

In diagram one, the circles are different sizes. This is deliberate. Mentoring is first and most important. The academic is valuable though secondary.

Why? If a person has been discipled but lacks knowledge, he will be motivated to pursue knowledge, even if he must educate himself with books alone. God will use him despite gaps in his knowledge.

What if a man has a dozen diplomas but is poorly discipled? What if his devotional life is lacking, his family in disarray and he disputes with his colleagues? His knowledge is no substitute.

THE ACADEMIC IS INDISPENSABLE THOUGH NOT PRIORITY

Certain mentors in the Bible wrote extensive books they expected successive generations to study and master. Moses, Paul and James were no anti-intellectuals. They were bright guys, who put a high value on scholarship.

Avoid influences that devalue the intellect. Such notions degrade the image of God in man, regardless of how much they may emphasize other aspects of Christian living or gifts. The academic is indispensable though not priority.

The mentor's toolbox

When we talk about mentoring relationships, we mean two specific areas in this order: Relationships with our colleagues, as we saw in Chapter Eighteen, then with those to whom we minister.

Precisely what does the mentor do? What methods does he employ?

Modeling and teaching

> **MODELING:** "Watch me do this. Then you do it also."

> **TEACHING:** "Here's why I do it this way and not some other way. The reason why you tried it and it did not work well was because...etc."

How do we translate theory into practice? Many theories propose answers. The Bible response, "a mentor."

Christ, the supreme leadership trainer, modeled how to cast out demons and heal the sick. Then he sent his disciples out to do it and it worked.

One day, they failed to cast out a particular demon. (Mk. 9:28,29) Then Jesus revealed this kind required a different approach...prayer.

This was an excellent didactic scenario. First, Jesus taught the basic procedure. Afterwards, he permitted an exception, modeling how to handle that as well.

Why is modeling effective? Learning becomes easier the more sensory faculties we employ. If we hear a fact, this involves only the ears. If we hear it and see it written, this engages both the eyes and the ears. If we hear it, see it, feel and talk about it, retention multiplies exponentially.

An example is the tangible impression Christ made on the Apostle John,

> *That which was from the beginning, which we have heard, which we have seen with our eyes, which we have looked at and our hands have touched — this we proclaim concerning the Word of life.* 1John 1:1

Elijah and Elisha were so similar in ministry style, I get confused about who did what. Is this similarity mere coincidence? I doubt it.

Elijah was the mentor, Elisha an attentive student. How do we know he was attentive? When Elijah was taken away to heaven, Elisha began to act just like him, with the same tone of authority.

With a good mentor, Elisha had a big head start and developed his own style later.

In the forum

Let's look in on three seminary students and a professor discussing the mentoring concept. The professor is Jay, also a respected and successful pastor. Bill, a student, works part time as an accountant and is studying for the pastorate. Jack is in his last semester and works as a youth pastor in a local church. He is a no-nonsense, athletic type. Susie is in her second year, a vivacious and quick-witted girl. The four are in a conference room, following a class with professor Jay.

"Hey, this sounds like catching smoke," Jack sighed, leaning forward. "I don't like ambiguities and the whole idea of relationships seems ambiguous to start with. Unless this mentoring thing takes form pretty soon, I'm out of here. Philosophy bores me."

Jay started to explain but Bill jumped in, "No really, Jack. I think I'm beginning to see where Jay is coming from. The idea of relationships seems fuzzy until we get into them. As a relationship develops, it stops being an idea and becomes a reality." Bill paused a moment, "In fact, it would seem the deeper and longer the relationship, the more concrete it becomes."

"It sounds to me like there's no quick way to prepare leaders," Susie interjected.

Jay chuckled, "And it sounds to me like you're getting the point, Susie."

"O.K., Jay, I'm starting to get it," Jack spoke up. "I have a question though. You said it was easy. But relationship building is not easy.

How do you square that with what you said before about mentoring being fundamentally easy?"

"Jack, I did not say it was *easy*. I said it was *simple*. I mean "simple" in its root idea. The process itself is anything but easy, because people are not simple."

"No shortcuts?" asked Susie.

"Oh sure, there's a shortcut. It is the one many take for preparing leaders. It's easier, quicker and represents no threat to anyone's ego. Want to hear what it is?"

Jack laughed, "I already know what you are going to say. Send them off somewhere to take a series of courses. You mentioned that before."

"Or even better," said Susie a bit sarcastically, "you can have them take correspondence courses."

Jack picked up on Susie's sarcasm and grinned. "That way they get credits and a diploma without having to interact with anybody. They have proof they have been "prepared" for leadership and can hang that proof on the wall."

Bill whispered loud enough for everyone to hear, "Jack's getting it."

"Hey, man, I got it at first. I talk it out to think it through. Courses, credits and diplomas are not really a shortcut. They're a way for both parties, leader and trainee, to avoid the time-consuming, ego-threatening process of relationships. That kind of training may seem good, but it leaves something out."

"Yeah," exclaimed Susie, "the *something* left out is Christianity!"

At this the whole group laughed. Jay put his hands on the table to signal he wanted their attention. "Maybe that exaggerates a bit, but it's close. It leaves out the heart and soul of Christianity...relationships! And what is a body without a heart and soul?"

The group replied almost simultaneously, "DEAD!" Everyone laughed.

The western concept

The groups' last comment exposes a fundamental defect in current leadership training today: The academic dominates.

Seminary catalogs describe leadership training as a series of 'courses.' Correspondence programs are also based on this same premise: "Take these courses and be prepared for Christian leadership!"

How did this mindset develop? The answer involves a difference in worldview. Eastern philosophy tends to be holistic. Eastern cultures view reality as a unit, spiritual and material blended. Western is more dualistic, seeing reality as two realms, spiritual and material.

This is why pantheism permeates eastern religions like Buddhism and Hinduism. Pantheism says everything is god. They do not mean God is everywhere. Pantheists assume a tree, a dog or a man is literally a part of 'god.'

Martial arts movies reflect eastern holistic thinking. These films often depict a close bond between the hero and a mentor who trained him in martial arts.

In simple terms, an eastern mindset claims the universe is one thing. A western philosophy regards it as two or more. Western thinking is also humanistic, focusing on the glory of man.

This dualism and humanism originated in ancient Greece. Alexander the Great conquered the ancient world and so did Greek humanism.

Greek philosophy assumed knowledge produces wisdom and virtue.

The Stoics supposed the study of nature would gain them insight into the meaning the universe and the force that sustains it. They failed.

THE INTELLECT IS ESSENTIAL BUT NOT CENTRAL

T he Bible contends wisdom is essentially relational... first with God and then with others. Acquiring knowledge is a part of wisdom, though not its foundation.

Intellect is essential but not central.

> *The fear of the LORD is the beginning of wisdom, and knowledge of the Holy One is understanding.* Proverbs 9:10

By the fifth century, Christianity dominated the western world. In the early middle ages, scholars became enamored with pre-Christian Greek culture. They referred to the Greek epoch, before the Roman conquests, as a "golden age." Greek philosophies seemed so profound, so right.

What if they could merge the best of Greek culture with Christianity? Wouldn't Christianity be the better for it? Surely a new golden age would be born. Scholars failed to consider the humanistic roots with its emphasis on man's intellect.

Medieval scholars invented the university system. Theology, accompanied by Greek and Roman classics, was required for everyone. If a young man aspired to be a doctor or a lawyer, he took courses.

What if a student desired to become a man of God? Likewise, he took courses to become a Christian leader. Was this successful? Hardly!

Bible schools and seminaries often do a commendable job of preparing Christians academically. However, these reflect the university system in a religious form with similar philosophical assumptions. They may inadvertently duplicate historic errors by reversing priorities.

The point: The Bible is an eastern book. Its message is holistic, without distinguishing secular from religious, spiritual from material. Biblical leadership training reflects this holistic worldview.

Leadership Training:

Biblical (rational) versus Western Philosophy (academic):

BIBLICAL	WESTERN TRADITION
Relational	*Academic*
Personal relationship with a mentor.	Relationship with teachers not essential. Some teachers even discourage relationships in order to remain 'objective.'
Wisdom is acquired through relationship with God and man.	Wisdom is acquired by knowledge, especially philosophy.
Teaching method: Modeling. (Do it like I did. Here's why we do it that way.)	Teaching method: A series of courses with professors. (Here's the theory, now go out on your own and try to put it into practice.)
Learn by doing	Learn by hearing
Theory and practice learned simultaneously through ministry.	Theory precedes practice.
Academic is essential but secondary.	Academic is all-important.

From this chapter we learn

- Biblical leadership training is a discipleship process involving a personal relationship between the mentor and the trainee. This is primarily relational via a mentoring process.

- Mentoring is holistic, comprising the whole person in all areas of his life.

- Mentoring is inseparable from the academic.

- The means for mentoring are modeling and teaching.

  - The mentor shows by example how to minister.

○ The mentor explains why he does things the way he does.

• The western concept of training focuses on the academic as priority.

• Western tradition places theory before practice, while biblical procedure makes theory and practice simultaneous via a mentor.

• Some schools claim they do leadership training when it is more accurate to describe it as academic training.

Study Questions for Chapter Nineteen

1. Describe the mentoring philosophy of leadership training.

2. What are the two tools of mentoring procedure and what do they entail?

3. What are the three aspects of mentoring described in this chapter.

4. What are some of the fundamental differences in assumptions between biblical leadership training and western tradition?

Chapter 20

Who Is Competent to Mentor?

Your call to biblical leadership embodies competence to mentor. Why? It's part of the package.

REMEMBER: The primary product of a Christian leader is other leader. This is a *major* part of your job description.

> *And the things you have heard me say in the presence of many witnesses entrust to reliable men who will also be qualified to teach others. 2Timothy 2:2*

So, if you are called to a biblical leadership office, such as pastor or elder, you are called to mentor.

Do you feel competent? Probably not. Wouldn't it be *nice* to feel competent? No. It would be arrogant. Even the Apostle Paul did not feel competent.

> Not that we are competent in ourselves to claim anything for ourselves, but our competence comes from God. (6) He has made us competent as ministers of a new covenant... 2Corinthians 3:5,6

"I will never be competent for any function in God's kingdom."

Like a tightrope walker with a balancing pole, we must hold to these two realities: —I will never be competent for any function in God's kingdom. —By the grace of God, I can do anything.

The issue is *call* not *competence.*

But by the grace of God I am what I am... 1Corinthians 15:10

Let's step into the forum again and observe the students struggling with the competence question:

"I have a confession to make, Jay," Bill said. "The idea of going up to somebody and saying I want to be their example of Christian living..."

Jack interrupted, "It sounds proud, Jay. Like I have it all together? I just got started in ministry and I'm going to be somebody else's model? Yea right!"

"Actually, the word 'proud' crossed my mind too," Bill agreed. "But I didn't want to say it outright."

Susie interjected, "You're polite."

Jack shook his head, "Come on, Susie, get serious."

"Hey, hear out the professor," she shot back. "I bet that's not the end of the story."

Bill interjected, "Let me tell you why I said that. I'm teaching a class on apologetics to a group of laymen. The truth is, I'm not so good at apologetics and I'm supposed to be the professor. I'm one chapter ahead of them in the book. Pray they don't find out I'm a fraud!"

Jay sat up. "You're not a fraud, Bill. Neither are any of us. In fact, if you felt any other way, I would be disappointed."

"But you've been around a while in ministry," Susie objected. "Like thirty years or something?"

"Thirty-eight to be exact. But let me tell you a secret. I'm still incompetent." Jay paused, "Not as incompetent as I was thirty-eight years ago. But I will die incompetent. Take another look at this verse. Paul declared he was incompetent also and I'm no Apostle Paul."

Jay read,

> *Such confidence as this is ours through Christ before God. (5) Not that we are competent in ourselves to claim anything for ourselves, but our competence comes from God. 2Corinthians 3:4,5*

Jay continued, "Paul's sense of competence came through his relationship with the Spirit, not because of his brains, experience or anything else. His personal walk with God, along with knowing what God had called him to do, was the ground on which he stood. He declared his dependence on God for his ability and then God used his brains and experience as the means to mentor."

Susie leaned back in her chair, "Yeah, that's a kingdom paradox for sure. We have to recognize our inability in order to be competent."

"Like we have to admit our dependence on the Lord to mentor correctly," Bill added. "There ought to be a name to describe this."

"Yes," Jay said, "it's called 'faith.' Remember what I said at the beginning of the course about God's grace for ministry?"

Jack replied, "Like 'there is no such thing as a job in the kingdom of God you are competent for. All of them work by grace.'"

"So...," Susie paused, "God is saying, 'You're incompetent. Now go do it.'"

"Exactly," Jay said, "now you guys go out and do it."

A predicament in South America

Still feeling inadequate? I hope so. It's hard to beat my experience in a small Latin American country with a fledgling denomination of about forty churches.

The leaders had discovered literature on reformed government and theology and loved it. They asked me to mentor the whole denomination in these two areas.

It struck me I was their first and only model of what a reformed minister should be. Was God joking? I almost asked him to send somebody else. Then I recalled Moses got into trouble for trying that.

How was I going to hide my faults so the nationals would not copy them? In the past, the only person who presumed I was good at concealing my faults was myself.

I've taught twice in that denomination in three cities and am still the only model they know. Yet they are growing. I do not know if God shrouded my faults or granted the nationals grace to ignore them. Either way, he used me, and they are on track.

Our faults are necessary

Thank God for the faults of Bible characters. Without them we would lack a well-rounded concept of ministry realities. God has a toolbox for perfecting his people. One of the tools is our faults.

The Lord does not count on our goodness to accomplish anything. He desires our willingness.

A chat between Jay, the professor and Jack the youth director, underlines the point:

"So, God overlooks our faults in the mentoring process and uses us anyway, right?" Jack questioned.

"More than overlook them, Jack. He uses them as tools in the process."

Jack rubbed the back of his neck thoughtfully. "Now that's a paradox if there ever was one. It gives me goose bumps."

"But it's liberating when you think about it, Jack. I used to think we had to be a really good guys to be a mentor."

"If God uses our faults as part of the program, then..." Jack hesitated. "Then we're free to be ourselves...like more authentic."

Jay smiled, "Now let me ask a question. Which kind of mentor would God most likely use...authentic or non authentic?"

Jack put his hand on his head, astonished, "Wow! That hurts! It sounds like you're saying God wants us to just be ourselves and let him use our faults to do the job."

"Let me tell you a secret about myself," Jay confided. "It took me a long time to quit being afraid of my faults when I'm mentoring."

"What you're implying is good news!"

"Actually, it's the *good news* of the gospel itself."

Do I have the anointing for this?

Assume the anointing is there and proceed accordingly. Why would God call us to ministry and not equip us for the job? The Bible tells us,

...the anointing you received from him remains in you...1John 2:27

...for God's gifts and his call are irrevocable. Romans 11:29

Do I have the right personality for training leaders?

A friend applied for service with a mission agency. Extensive psychological testing, along with an interview with a psychologist, was part of the application process.

During the interview the psychologist said, "I regret to tell you that your psychological test shows you are not apt for missionary service. I cannot recommend you to the mission board."

The psychologist was unaware my friend had served as a missionary for 25 years, was instrumental in planting several churches, had been a field and team leader in two countries and had trained many for the ministry.

The next day, when my friend appeared before the mission board, the moderator said, "You realize the mission psychologist did not recommend you. We have learned to take his recommendations lightly. We look more at experience and accomplishment. Welcome to the family."

THE BIBLE UNDERSCORES VIRTUE.
THE   WORLD   VALUES
PERSONALITY.

For decades, corporations embraced the latest psychological theories about management. Psychological profiling is still mandatory in many large businesses before appointment to leadership.

Profiling influences Christian organizations as well. This trend is just that...a trend.

Contemporary research into business management shows no relationship between personality types and success. Instead, key virtues make personality differences irrelevant.

Integrity, the courage to take risks and total commitment to a vision make personality typing secondary. Any given personality, however extroverted, strong willed or forceful, will fail in leadership if lacking these qualities.

Management studies have discovered quiet types zipped past some aggressive personalities and outperformed them...IF they possessed the above character qualities.

The Bible underscores virtue. The world values personality.

How will my trainees recognize my call to mentor them?

In Ecuador, a student displayed a hostile attitude during a course I was teaching. He would ask feisty questions in a disrespectful tone. As a professor, I welcome questions. This student, a civil engineer in his late 30's named José, clearly disliked me as well as the subject I was teaching.

A year and half later, my wife ran into him at a grocery store. He expressed he wished to visit me and insisted it was important.

He sat on our couch and said...

"Do you remember your class I attended?"

"Yes," I replied.

"I gave you a rough time. I'm here to repent for the sin I committed against you."

It seemed he was too serious, when a simple apology would do. But he continued...

"Let me tell you what happened. Since I saw you last, I lost my job, my house and nearly lost my family. I was falsely accused of fraud and almost landed in jail. I have been cleared, but asked God why he allowed these things. He showed me I was arrogant and proud, self-sufficient and independent. He reminded me of the way I treated you in class.

"José, I forgive you."

"One more thing, before I finish," he said. "God told me I should sit at your feet and learn."

"If your pastor is in agreement, I'll do it."

"He is," José replied. "I already asked him."

For a year I mentored José in Christian leadership. He was an excellent student and was ordained as an elder in his church shortly thereafter.

Incidents like these are rare. Usually, the mentoring process occurs in more natural ways. It illustrates in a dramatic way, however, the answer to the question: How will our trainees recognize God has made us competent to mentor them? Answer: Don't worry about it. One way or another, God himself will tell them.

From this chapter we learn

- Anyone called to a biblical leadership office, such as pastor or elder, is called to mentor.

- We need the grace of God to mentor, just as in other areas.

- People who *feel* competent to mentor probably should not do it.

- Personality types have nothing to do with success in mentoring, managing or leadership in general.

- Our faults are not a hindrance to mentoring because God employs them as part of the process.

- We assume we possess the anointing of the Holy Spirit for mentoring because God always bestows anointing with the call.

- God himself will tell your trainee to submit to your leadership.

Study Questions for Chapter Twenty

1. How do we know if we are called to mentor others for leadership?

2. What makes us competent to mentor?

3. Describe the role our faults play in the mentoring process.

4. What is the relationship between personality type and effectiveness as leader? Why?

5. Describe the weakness in psychological testing as a criterion for determining leadership competence.

Chapter 21

The Mentoring Covenant

I n the previous chapter I mentioned José who God humbled and came for mentoring. We had an informal agreement.

In contrast, a young minister in Ecuador named Ricardo from another denomination asked to join our movement because of a change in his theology. The Presbytery appointed me to mentor Ricardo in Presbyterian government and practical leadership style.

This particular mentoring situation was formal. The mentoring arrangement was initiated by the Presbytery and recorded in the official minutes.

In yet a third circumstance, a medical doctor desired ordination in our denomination. It happened we were good friends and worked together on several projects. In retrospect, mentoring was occurring naturally.

This third example was informal, unwritten and initiated by God himself.

Each of these mentoring opportunities required a different approach. The result was the same. All three candidates were eventually ordained.

The mentoring relationship may be formal or informal, conscious or assumed. Either party can initiate it. However, it happens, a mentoring covenant is an agreement between a mentor and a trainee about the training process.

A MENTORING COVENANT IS AN AGREEMENT BETWEEN A MENTOR AND A TRAINEE ABOUT THE TRAINING PROCESS.

All relationships have rules

E ven the most casual relationships between neighbors include certain unspoken rules about respect of property and privacy. Relationships, like marriage, include more extensive rules.

Mentoring in leadership also involves rules. It is helpful to define the rules since leadership preparation includes private life.

If the relationship is formal, you may need to write out the rules. If your relationship with the trainee is informal and has already existed this may not be necessary.

In our Visión R.E.A.L training system, we clearly articulate the rules:

- The mentor and trainee will meet at least once a month to discuss the mentoring process...problems and plans in ministry.

- Every trainee will have a ministry assigned to him to develop.

- The mentor will evaluate the trainee every three months, in all areas of life, using an evaluation form we provide. This will require vulnerability and openness.

The mentoring covenant therefore contains a mutual commitment: Both agree to be candid. The trainee agrees to correction and instruction in every area of life, not just ministerial performance. The mentor agrees to caring and training in a nurturing manner.

Commitment to change

Have you ever met a person committed to remaining exactly the same? We each have a certain natural resistance to change. Some people though, seem to make a point of it. The trainee therefore must be committed to change in all areas of his life if he expects to attain to leadership.

Tip: In local church situations, avoid telling people you are training them for leadership. It is better to say you are preparing them to serve the Lord according to their gifts.

In Ecuador, we created a serious problem when we appointed a dynamic businessman as a leadership candidate. We were sure his skills in business would transfer smoothly into a church setting.

Arrogance and unwillingness to accept correction eventually required removing his candidature. He regarded this as public humiliation and he tried to avenge himself by slandering the leadership among church members. His real motive for leadership was for his own honor, not the honor of Christ.

If you cannot avoid letting the person know he is a leadership candidate, at least try not to advertise it broadly in case of failure.

Who do you select as trainees?

Our missionary team in Latin America had a silver-tongued young national named David lined up as pastoral candidate. An immature field leader had appointed him as a candidate, without consulting the team. Since David did not have a job, the leader promised him a scholarship out of the team's budget.

David was habitually late. He never completed a single assignment, and his excuses were creative. He was the kind of persuasive guy who could sell sand to Arabs.

One day his pastor pleaded, "Brother Roger, *please* help us remove David as a leadership candidate. He accomplishes nothing and condemns the leadership for all own faults. We've struggled with this man for five years and he is still unreliable."

Principle one: Faithfulness

Is it our job as mentors to make unfaithful men faithful? The Apostle Paul, in 1 Timothy, narrows the prospects for leadership to faithful men.

I discussed this point with a missionary on our team. He wanted to ordain four men right away, without going through the training established by the church planting team.

"Roger," he said, "all the scriptures require for ordination is good character."

"Where do you get that idea, Sam?" I asked.

"In First Timothy, Paul talks about faithful character as a condition for ordination. We don't need anything more than that. "

"Sam, take a look again at the text. Paul says, *They must first be tested,* He does not say 'ordain them as soon as they have good character.' He says 'take men of good character and then train them.' The qualifications in First Timothy are NOT qualifications for ordination. They are qualifications for *candidacy.*"

"Well then, where are the qualifications for elders if not those?" Sam asked sarcastically.

"The rest of the pastoral epistles are the qualifications. Those epistles tell us all elders must be able to evangelize, refute false doctrine and other duties. The character qualifications in First Timothy Three are simply the skeleton on which these other leadership aspects hang. Character alone does not qualify them."

Sam eventually conceded the point.

Faithfulness is foremost. However gifted your trainee, if his character is unstable, he is not teachable. No matter how talented, he is disqualified as a candidate.

Principle number one in selecting a trainee is therefore:

———— ◄O► ————

SELECT FOR FAITHFULNESS

———— ◄O► ————

Principle two: Openness and vulnerability

At a missionary training school in London where I ministered, we had a new missionary arrive. He and his wife lived in an upstairs apartment. One day I had to ask him about something. I knocked on the door and the door opened about three inches, only an eye visible.

During the entire conversation, the door opened not a centimeter further. I ignored this incident because I assumed his wife might be dressing or resting. This occurred so regularly, that others noticed it.

This reflected his personality. His private life was closed to everyone. Ministry for him was a day job. He accomplished next to nothing and left the ministry after one term on the field.

In contrast, we visited a missionary family in Argentina ministering to youth. Their door was wide open. Young people were going in and out. A young man from out of town who had been there for three weeks occupied one of the guest rooms.

I asked the missionary's wife, "How do you ever get any privacy?" She laughed, "Privacy? What's that?"

During the four days we were there, a young man from a dysfunctional family said, "Before I met the Smiths, I had decided to never marry. To me, family life was a nightmare. I've changed my mind. Now I know what a real family can be like."

The Smith family's home reflected their open hearts. Remember: *Leadership and privacy do not mix.*

At some point, you as mentor must make it clear that the mentoring process will involve every area of their life. This includes family life, relationship with colleagues, personal quiet time and ministry competence.

To some people, this may feel intrusive. If you show concern for their welfare and respect for their persons, they will not take it as such.

Mentoring covenant involves mutual vulnerability.

MENTORING INVOLVES MUTUAL VULNERABILITY

Openness is mutual

We cannot expect others to open their lives and hearts to us unless we do the same. Like the two missionary couples above, one successful, the other not, the difference was in openness and vulnerability to others.

TIP: Beware of *Mr. Incognito*

This is the type of person you can only contact if he wants it. He arranges his life so no one can contact him unless he chose to be reached. You call at his house and no one answers, so you leave a message. You never know where he is. Their entire demeanor says, "don't call me, I'll call you."

This kind of person decides whether contact takes place or not. Mr. Incognitos are disqualified for ministry, especially leadership. The reason is not just a bad habit or peculiarity of temperament. Mr. Incognitos do not really care about people.

If your candidate is a Mr. Incognito, you may want to calculate whether or not you will be able to bring him out of this syndrome. If not, go ahead and give him work, but not ordination.

Principle number two in selecting a trainee is therefore:

————————◆O◆————————

SELECT FOR OPENNESS AND VULNERABILITY.

————————◆O◆————————

Principle three: Self-starters

What were the disciples doing when Jesus first met them? Sitting around waiting for somebody to tell them what to do? No. They were working.

Some had their own businesses, such as fishing or tax collecting. Jesus did not go to the marketplace to recruit people standing around looking for work. He found people we call today, *proactive.* This means self-starters, men with initiative who did not need someone to light a fire under them to get them to produce.

Before meeting Christ, Simon the Zealot belonged to an anti-Roman movement, which taught that violence, was legitimate. "Zealot" was the name of this movement. He had vision and zeal for political change.

While Simon was trying to figure how best to kill Romans, Matthew was starting his own tax collecting business. Peter was running a fishing outfit.

Christ did nothing to quench Simon's vision and zeal. He simply redirected it to God's purpose. Nor did he stop Matthew from collecting. He merely taught him to collect something other than taxes...souls. Neither did he hinder Peter from catching fish. He just taught him to catch two-legged ones.

These were men on the move. Each ended up with a vision for God's glory and the advancement of his kingdom.

Initiative! Drive! Instilling vision in proactive people is not particularly difficult.

The point? Rarely do we observe people with vision just letting life happen. The key distinction between an ordinary Christian worker and a genuine leader is *vision*...a burning desire to accomplish something significant for God. Vision is usually born out of the hearts of self-starters.

Principle number 3 in selecting a trainee is therefore:

———◈———

SELECT SELF-STARTERS.

———◈———

Principle four: Giftedness

The Bible speaks a great deal about gifts for ministry. Experience is important but giftedness is indispensable.

God called and gifted Jeremiah as a prophet. Though he had no experience, God told him to confront the elders of Israel.

The Lord told him to ignore his own youthful appearance. (Jeremiah 1:5-9) Jewish custom looked to seniority when it came to protocol in addressing a group. Likewise, Paul told Timothy not to let others despise his youth. (1 Timothy 4:12) We know nothing of the age difference between Timothy and his leadership trainees. Some may have been older than he.

Suppose you must choose between two candidates to teach the adult Sunday school class. One has had experience but no clear gift of teaching. The other is a gifted teacher but has never taught an adult Sunday school class. Which do you choose?

Choose the gifted. Though he will make errors at first, he will learn fast and soon surpass the other. It's like two runners, one which of has a head starts but is slower. Given time, the faster will win.

Experience alone rarely rises above mediocrity. To have excellence in your ministry, you must first select on the basis of talent and gifts. The combination of talent plus experience is the dynamite that will make your movement grow. If you fail to follow this principle, you will condemn your movement to mediocrity.

Principle number four in selecting a trainee is therefore:

SELECT FOR GIFTEDNESS

Pitfalls in mentoring

Beware of cloning

I admit a fault: I have a strong desire for my students to be theologians and writers. I'm glad it won't happen. It would make for a boring world.

It's a common tendency for mentors to want their trainees to be like them. Your job as a mentor is to make your trainee more of what he already is, not more of what you are. Your job is to discover his gift and help him develop it, regardless of whether you have the same gift or not.

Avoid rules

When you assign ministry to your trainee, avoid giving him a lot of rules. You take away his ability to make choices and be creative, frustrating the mentoring process. Let him do the job his way, within the general parameters you proscribe.

No leftovers

Do not let anyone dump on your candidate scraps of ministry nobody else wants. When you assign him a ministry, make sure it is worthwhile and fulfilling.

Well-rounded nonsense

A fallacy in leadership training is making candidates focus on weak areas so they will be well-rounded. The only well-rounded ministers in history were the apostles and they are dead. Focus on your candidates' strengths and make them stronger.

Christ taught this principle,

> Whoever has will be given more, and he will have an abundance. Matthew 12:13

From this chapter we learn

- A mentoring covenant is an agreement between a mentor and a trainee as to the procedures in the training process.

- The mentoring covenant involves mutual openness.

- In choosing trainees for leadership we select for...

  ○ Faithfulness

  ○ Openness and vulnerability

  ○ Initiative

  ○ Giftedness

- We must beware of common pitfalls in mentoring.

  ○ Trying to make the trainee like ourselves.

  ○ Supervising too closely.

  ○ Assigning ministry scraps.

  ○ Focusing on his weaknesses rather than strengths.

Study Questions for Chapter Twenty-One

1. Describe what is meant by *mutual vulnerability*.

2. Describe the criteria mentioned here for selecting trainees.

3. Explain why giftedness is secondary to experience in selecting trainees.

4. Describe at least two pitfalls in mentoring, plus one you may have observed or experienced which is not mentioned in this chapter.

Conclusion

C hristian leaders deal with weighty matters involving the lives of God's people. To float a heavy object, we must have something underneath to sustain it. A brick will float if it is resting on a board. So it is with leadership. The "board" is our personal integrity and humility before God and man. We can float a lot of weight on that. Without it, we are sunk. People learn quickly if our integrity has a sellout price. Without this principal virtue, our leadership is crippled. With it, other elements fall naturally into line.

Christian leadership is fundamentally simple if we remember this central truth. The quality of our personal walk with God has more to do with leadership than managerial techniques.

The world's paradigms constantly shift. Christ modeled only one leadership paradigm which has never changed: Integrity, a disposition to embrace suffering, treating others with respect as God's image and dealing with our fellow ministers as equals along with a servant attitude.

It is dangerous for Christian organizations to emulate the world's organizational structures and mind set. Most become authoritarian hierarchies, which are the antithesis of Christian leadership. Such structures bring out the worst us: Arrogance, authoritarianism, jealousy and incompetence. To mitigate the damage, the world must invent a plethora of managerial techniques to get by.

Good communication between leaders and their subordinates is a key to success. Followers need to feel they are valued as persons and can express their views without fear of reprisal.

A leader must have *vision*. A vision is an attainable goal of great importance involving intense commitment. Without this, a person may be a manager, but not a leader. Likewise, a leader must be able to do realistic planning, with intermediate goals. Without planning he is merely a visionary.

Finally, a leader needs to keep in mind that God's call gives him privileges and authority to do his job even though he is a servant. As with other aspects of Christian living, he lives in paradox. He is a slave with authority, a servant who directs. He attributes his accomplishments to Christ and views his greatest honor in terms of bringing glory to Him alone.

Appendix

Peter Principles

(From the book **THE PETER PRINCIPLE**
by Dr. Lawrence Peters, Sociologist)

In his classic, The Peter Principle, sociologist Dr. Peters outlines the dynamics of a hierarchy and how it produces inefficiency. Below are the problems he has observed in his study of hierarchies.

1. Every employee rises to his level of incompetence.

2. Any productive employee has not reached his level of incompetence.

3. Super-competent employees will be fired. They represent a threat to the stability of the hierarchy, which is the supreme value of a hierarchy.

4. Contrary to popular belief, production is not the supreme value. Stability is.

5. "Pull" is more important that "push". Pull means being favored by superiors. Push means trying harder to do a good job, or self-improvement.

6. Downward pressure of seniority always neutralizes "push." To the hierarchy, he who has been around longest has more chance

of promotion that the employee who is better qualified. The employee whom the superiors happen to like, for whatever reason, has the best chance of all. Qualifications do not necessarily matter.

7. Being a good follower is guaranteed to make you a poor leader.

8. In a hierarchy, creativity and innovativeness will be viewed as incompetence.

9. Leadership potential may be viewed as insubordination in a hierarchy.

10. Higher level incompetent officials are rarely aware of their incompetence.

11. Higher echelon officials will always project the impression they are   wise and have things in control. This is not necessarily so.

Bibliography

A dams, Jay. **COMPETENT TO COUNSEL.**

Adam's work on Christian counseling is a classic. He takes, however, a very controversial stand when it comes to psychological issues. He feels all psychological problems, apart from physiological damage to the brain, are caused by sin in some form. Since a lot of psychological problems are indeed caused by sin, this book can help the Christian leader to get to the bottom of issues. Adams deals quite a bit with the human tendency toward blame shifting. 320 pages.

Anderson, Neil. **BONDAGE BREAKER.**

This has been a popular book for dealing with the demonic power in the life of those with serious sin addictions. Anderson rejects approaches that directly confront demonic powers, opting for inserting truth into the mind and heart of the individual along with thorough confession and repentance. The book has been rejected in some Reformed circles because his doctrine of man is defective. If the reader ignores Anderson's weak anthropology, the rest of the book is useful. 302 pages.

Blanchard, Kenneth. **ONE MINUTE MANAGER.**

This remarkable little book lays out simple principles by which a leader can create a positive atmosphere in the workplace. Blanchard focuses on positive reinforcement in relating to subordinates. 112 pages.

Blanchard and Zigarmi. **LEADERSHIP AND THE ONE MINUTE MANAGER.**

The sequel to One Minute Manager. Blanchard refines his positive reinforcement techniques with an emphasis on how different leadership styles affect the way his principles are applied. He identifies four styles along with the way distinct types of people need different "strokes." 112 pages.

Bonhoeffer, Dietrich. **THE COST OF DISCIPLESHIP**

This late German theologian's challenge is appropriate for Christian leadership. Becoming a Christian leader entails becoming a committed disciple, devoted to the cross and the suffering a cross implies. 316 pages.

Buckingham and Coffman. **FIRST, BREAK ALL THE RULES**

The subtitle is *what the world's greatest managers do differently.* Buckingham works for Gallup Poll, which did twenty years of research into what makes great management tick. The results explode common beliefs about effective management.

Charnock, Stephen. **EXISTENCE AND ATTRIBUTES OF GOD**

The outstanding classic on God's attributes. The section on holiness is thorough and profoundly convicting. This can be a resource for the leader in helping people see why sin is an offense to God and not merely an inconvenience. 542 pages.

Crabb, Larry. **FINDING GOD**

Crabb is a well-known Christian psychologist. This book is a portrayal of his personal struggle with tragedy issues, along with his own sinful attitudes and how God brought him out of it. A Christian leader may find this appropriate for some believers struggling with sin issues. 240 pages.

Clinton, Robert. **THE MAKING OF A LEADER**

This author claims he has identified six stages God uses to develop a leader. He bases his views on his studies of hundreds of figures throughout history. He helps the reader identify where he is in this process. 272 pages.

Collins, Jim. **GOOD TO GREAT.**

Latest research on leadership qualities of company executives who attained to great success while others in the same field failed. Collins was surprised at his own findings. Humility and passionate commitment, characterizes these leaders. Well worth the price. 300 pages.

Covey, Stephen. **PRINCIPLE CENTERED LEADERSHIP.**

Addresses the differences between "tough" hardball management and "kind" softball management. Covey shows how to transcend both by a third alternative that it both tougher and kinder. 336 pages.

Covey, Stephen. **SEVEN HABITS OF EFFECTIVE PEOPLE.**

This businessman has done an in-depth study on the personal character attributes of successful people in various domains. Mainly directed toward businessmen, it focuses on certain mental and emotional habits that make them effective leaders. Though Covey is not an Evangelical, it is remarkable how close he comes to scriptural principles. 319 pages.

Elgin, Susanne. **THE GENTLE ART OF VERBAL SELF DEFENSE.**

Elgin, a psychologist, teaches techniques for dealing with people who are verbal aggressors or habitually critical. These techniques are a verbal judo that deflects the attack without becoming aggressive. 310 pages.

Fisher, Ury and Patton. **GETTING TO YES.**

The sequel to Getting Past No. These authors take a more positive approach to negotiation than in the first book, focusing on avoiding what they call "positional" confrontations and changing it to "situational" negotiation. 200 pages.

Ford, Leighton. **TRANSFORMING LEADERSHIP.**

One of the few books that rightly focuses on Jesus himself as the ultimate model of leadership. Ford takes insights from Christ's character as he interacts with His generation in a variety of situations. He examines Jesus as servant, shepherd, defender against legalists, etc.

It is provocative, in that it seeks to combine the insights from various references to the character and context of the situations that Jesus and his disciples found themselves in. 320 pages

Getz, Gene. **THE MEASURE OF A MAN.**

Useful for small group study in Christian character in leadership. Getz bases his teaching on the qualifications for eldership from 1 Timothy 3. He takes each character concept and amplifies it, challenging the students to discuss how they may apply it within their own context. 197 pages.

Hendricks, Howard. **SEVEN LAWS OF THE TEACHER.**

Since much of Christian leadership is involved with teaching, this book is useful. Hendricks emphasizes the personal commitment of the teacher to the student beyond his role as a mere dispenser of knowledge. 180 pages.

Hession, Roy. **CALVARY ROAD.**

This little book has been appreciated for years as an excellent treatise on repentance in the life of the believer. Hession, however, seems to base his thinking on the assumption there is no forgiveness for a sin unless we confess it to God. This shows a shallow understanding of the quantity and depth of sin remaining in the nature of the believer. Hession corrected this defect in a subsequent book. Apart from this, the book is worthwhile. 120 pages.

Hock, Dee. **AGE OF THE CHAORDIC.**

Hock is the founder of Visa credit card, the biggest business enterprise in history. He takes his premise from nature, which produces order out of chaos through competition. Leaders must not, therefore, fear either chaos or competition. They must deliberately allow organizational structure to be loose enough to risk chaos in order to gain creativity and innovation from their employees. This book revolutionizes thinking about management. It is invaluable. 345 pages.

Janowski and Shapiro. **THE POWER OF NICE: HOW TO NEGOTIATE SO EVERYONE WINS.**

A leader in the win-win theory of negotiation. The authors explore techniques for "building bridges" during negotiation so everyone feels they have "won." 304 pages.

Kotter, John. **LEADING CHANGE.**

Researcher Kotter has "discovered" that autocratic leadership rarely works well in any context and tends toward counterproductively in the long run. He explains methods for bringing change within an organization without abusing one's authority. 187 pages.

Loeb and Kindle. **LEADERSHIP FOR DUMMIES.**

The humorous title belies some of the most common sense principles of leadership ever written. This book inspired some of the ideas in the student's manual on Vision and Goals. It is immensely practical. 358 pages.

Martin-Lloyd Jones. **SPIRITUAL DEPRESSION.**

THE CLASSIC ON DEPRESSION IN THE LIFE OF THE BELIEVER. AMONG OTHER TOPICS, JONES DEALS WITH DEPRESSION CAUSED BY HABITUAL SIN AND THE INABILITY TO OVERCOME IT. JONES' WRITING STYLE IS PADDED, SOMEWHAT TEDIOUS. IT COULD BE REDUCED BY A THIRD WITHOUT INJURY TO CONTENT. 300 PAGES.

Maxwell, John. **THE 21 IRREFUTABLE LAWS OF LEADERSHIP.**

The author lays out 21 characteristics of leaders. The list seemed tedious. One tends to ask, "Who can remember all these, let alone live them?" Nevertheless, they are good tips, though slanted toward American culture. 256 pages.

Mumford, Bob. **GUIDANCE.**

Mumford is an Assembly of God minister. His book on guidance covers the key "signs" in the life of the believer: the Word, circumstances, godly counsel and so forth. Because of his Pentecostal leanings, the book exudes a certain mystical flavor that may be annoying to some Reformed readers. Helpful in decision-making for leaders since this is a question of divine guidance anyway. 156 pages.

Orr, Robert. **LEADERSHIP ESSENTIALS.**

This large book is one of the most complete studies in leadership available. It contains numerous graphics, some humorous. It covers all aspects of leadership in most situations in which a Christian leader is likely to find himself. Orr is a former missionary to Latin America, dedicated to training nationals. His sensitivity to the needs of nationals makes his book apropos for study by nationals. 532 pages.

Peter, Lawrence. **THE PETER PRINCIPLE.**

This book is the classic on dynamics of hierarchical structures. Peter is a sociologist who discovered and described the now famous principle that an employee in a hierarchy will tend to rise to his level of incompetence. This produces mediocrity in the organization. This humorous and entertaining book is a must for anyone wanting to understand dynamics of an organization. 192 pages.

Peter, Lawrence. **PETER PRINCIPLE REVISITED.**

Times have changed since Dr. Peter first published *The Peter Principle.* This update includes new illustrations and incorporates how hierarchies have attempted to mitigate their own incompetence in a competitive world. 207 pages.

Philipps, Donald. **LINCOLN ON LEADERSHIP.**

When Philipps did his dissertation for his master's in business administration, he chose President Abraham Lincoln as the background for leadership principles. He considers Lincoln the greatest leader the western world has ever seen. Lincoln was a Christian. Though the book is not overtly "Christian," the principles are excellent for leadership in a Christian context. It is the best I have ever read on leadership principles in general. 188 pages.

Piper, John. **BROTHERS, WE ARE NOT PROFESSIONALS.**

Piper's book is a series of exhortations to his fellow ministers. It starts with a call to a ministry focus that disregards the expectations of society of what a pastor is supposed to be and aims toward radical discipleship. The book seems to meander through a variety of topics, all of which are legitimate. One gets the impression, however, that Piper has used the book as a catchall for his miscellaneous opinions on what a minister should do and be. 150 pages.

Ramsey, Richard. **HOW GOOD MUST I BE?**

For new believers falling into the sin of legalism, whether from false teaching or the zeal of repentance, this little study guide is helpful without being preaching. Ramsey uses an oblique approach to undermining a works righteousness mentality. 102 pages.

Sanders, Oswald. **SPIRITUAL LEADERSHIP.**

Possibly the best text ever written on the character development of a Christian leader. The book contains few managerial principles because Sanders focuses on spiritual and moral qualities necessary to attract followers. 189 pages.

Spence, Gerry. **HOW TO ARGUE AND WIN EVERY TIME.**

Spence is the world's most successful defense lawyer in history. He has never lost a case. The catchy title belies serious principles to help a person "embody" his message. These include "passionate commitment" to one's subject, accompanied with thorough knowledge of the facts of the argument. He rejects "cold" objectivity for ardent confidence in the justice of one's cause. 307 pages.

Sproul, R.C. **HOLINESS OF GOD.**

For Christians under the noetic effect of sin, with a shallow understanding of the gravity of their condition, Sproul's book may be convicting. It avoids the tediousness of, while theologically sound. 234 pages

Tozer, A.W. **KNOWLEDGE OF THE HOLY.**

A classic on introduction to the attributes of God in general. The section on holiness was very good, without appearing overly exhortatory. 128 pages.

Tjosvold, Dean. **Learning to Manage Conflict.**

This professional negotiator uses the concept of "cooperative conflict."
This amounts to a kind of verbal judo to avoid direct confrontation to
arrive at a win-win situation. This book inspires some of the negotiation
techniques used in my manual. 176 pages.

Ury, William. **Getting Past No.**

The classic on difficult negotiation situations. These professional
negotiators show how to deal with difficult or hostile people with whom
we must negotiate for one reason or another. These include the guy
who considers himself a "tough negotiator," in win-lose situation. They
identify techniques to turn the issue to a common problem both parties
need to resolve. 189 pages.

Van Oech, Roger. **A Whack on the Side of the Head.**

This creative little book was the inspiration behind the chapter on creative
thinking. With comical graphics and charming style, it whacks the reader
in a way that makes him want to think more creatively. 141 pages.

White, John. **Excellence in Leadership**

The author uses Nehemiah as the model for the kinds of stress and
opposition a Christian faces. He focuses on prayer as the antidote for
personal attacks, internal opposition and seeming lack of resources. 132
pages.

Watson, Thomas. **The Doctrine of Repentance.**

A classic of puritan theology on repentance, published 1668. Like a typical
puritan of the epic, Watson is thorough and somewhat tedious to read.
For those interested in the history of thought on repentance in Reformed
circles, this book is a good place to start. 122 pages.

www.ingramcontent.com/pod-product-compliance
Lightning Source LLC
Chambersburg PA
CBHW072347090426
42741CB00012B/2957